A
PRIMER OF HERALDRY
FOR AMERICANS

BY

EDWARD S. HOLDEN, LL.D.

NEW YORK
THE CENTURY CO.
1898

THE DE VINNE PRESS

Book-plate (arms) of
President George Washington.

TO M·M AND E·H

TABLE OF CONTENTS

INTRODUCTORY NOTE

IT is usual to commence American books on heraldic and genealogic matters with a half-apology for introducing such subjects to the notice of the citizens of a republic. The writer believes apologies to be entirely unnecessary. Such topics deserve their due share of attention (though it may not be a large share) in a country which contains millions of descendants of good families of England and the Continent. General George Washington inherited a coat of arms from reputable English ancestors, and used it on appropriate occasions. Benjamin Franklin applied for and obtained a grant of armorial bearings, and his motto was, *Exemplum adest ipse homo* (" Conduct marks the man "). Where two such Republicans led, Americans need not fear to follow.

The writer began his heraldic studies as a school-boy with Scott's novels and Froissart's Chronicles. The present book has been written at spare moments, as a relief from very different work. The information that it contains will help to solve many enigmas in Architecture, Art, Literature, and History (both European and colonial), and will enable the reader to take an intimate pleasure in matters that otherwise are merely puzzling and, at first sight, repellent. Much of our mother-literature (especially Shakspere, Scott, Tennyson, etc.), and very much of foreign literature (Ariosto, Tasso, Froissart, etc.), cannot be intelligently read without a little learning of the sort. Gothic Architecture tells no story, and Painting often tells an incomplete one, without some rudiments of heraldic knowledge. Half the point of History is lost unless it is studied in its details. To comprehend its details (especially in the period from the Crusades to the French Revolution) an accurate knowledge of heraldry is a material aid. La Bruyère, in his " Caractères " (De la Ville), enumerates the uses to which armorial bearings were put in his day (1688). "They are emblazoned everywhere," he says: "on stained-glass windows, over the doors, even on the locks, on coaches, and on liveries." What was true in 1688 is also true to-day. The seals of countries, provinces, and states are heraldic; so are their flags. Coins and medals are stamped with heraldic emblems; each government department or office has its seal; cities, corporations, colleges, universities, employ seals and devices, as do societies and individuals. Heraldry is a doctrine which has to do with all these things, and it is interesting and advantageous to know something of it. The visiting-cards of foreigners—counts, barons, *Freiherren*—bear their coronets, and the rank and title can be decided at a glance. Note-paper is similarly marked, and the sex and condition of the writer can be discovered from the coat of arms.

As such devices are in every-day use in this country, and still more in foreign countries, it is worth while to understand the universal rules according to which they are employed, and not to make blunders that may easily be avoided. Not to follow these rules is simply to refuse to admit the alphabet of the language which one is employing. For instance, no woman except a queen may bear a crest. Let American ladies remember this simple rule in ordering their book-plates and stationery. No unmarried woman may bear arms on a knight's shield. Since A. D. 1350 (except on American letter-paper) such arms have been borne on a lozenge ($\lozenge$).

The present little book treats of such matters in a compact form and a simple manner, and it is fully illustrated. Its materials have been gathered from leisurely and extensive reading, not only in English but in continental heraldry; and some of them, at least, will be new to most Americans. It will serve as a primer for young people, and as a handy book of reference to their elders; and it should be especially useful to the members of the many hereditary patriotic societies now formed, and forming, throughout the country. Special attention is here paid to such organizations, and it is believed that a perusal of this book will make the reader a better, not a worse, American.

E. S. H.

New York, January, 1898.

A PRIMER OF HERALDRY
FOR AMERICANS

A PRIMER OF HERALDRY
FOR AMERICANS

ARMS (or armorial bearings) are hereditary heraldic devices, arranged according
to conventional rules, appertaining to and
honorably distinctive of individuals, corporations, cities, countries, etc. They are
usually blazoned (painted in color) on a
shield, and surmounted by a helmet and
crest, and they may be accompanied by
supporters, mottos, and mantlings. An
achievement of arms is the aggregate of all
these devices as borne by a person; so
called because in old days the honor of
arms was achieved by knightly deeds.
Heraldry (or armory) is the body of doctrine (it used to be ranked as a science)
which prescribes the rules by which arms

1

are composed; in its widest scope it has to do with honorary distinctions of all kinds. The business of the herald, as Dr. Johnson well says, "is to proclaim peace and to denounce war; to be employed in martial messages; and to judge and examine coats of arms."

EMBLEMS

THE tribes of Israel had their distinctive emblems—Judah its lion. Æschylus, Herodotus, and many ancient writers describe the devices borne on the shields of warriors. Such devices were more than mere ornament, and partook of the nature of personal badges; but they were not hereditary, as armorial bearings are. Alexander the Great distributed such special distinctions among his generals, precisely as Napoleon granted arms to his marshals. Trajan's Column in Rome was erected in the years A. D. 98--117, and the shields of the Dacians sculptured upon it are covered with emblems, as the sun, the moon, etc. Even our Red Indian clans were distinguished by totemic signs, and each individual warrior had his personal cognizance. From remote antiquity nations and tribes have employed devices and insignia, which were often displayed on their standards, banners, etc. The eagle of the Roman Empire is a familiar example. The white horse was borne by the Saxons from the earliest times, and it is to-day the cognizance of the house of Hanover; it was the emblem used by Alfred the Great (died 901). The kingdom of Wessex bore a golden dragon. The wivern was the emblem of the Vandals; the raven that of the Danes. The wolf was the emblem of the city of Rome; the horse's head that of Carthage; the olive-branch and the owl those of Athens. So far as is known, these devices were not emblazoned on shields; but they were the forerunners of true heraldic charges. Pope Benedict VIII (1013) presented to the Emperor Henry II, at his coronation, a globe surmounted by a cross, as an emblem of the power of the cross over the world. In later times this became the symbol of imperial or royal power among Christian nations (see Fig. 66).

Such emblems among European nations laid the foundation for true heraldry. The arms of the knight were borne upon his shield, oftentimes repeated in his crest, painted on his banner, sculptured on his castle and on his tomb, and finally became a precious inheritance to his descendants. Here we have the marks of veritable *arms* as distinguished from non-hereditary emblems. Emblems were personal badges, and were not necessarily inherited. Arms are hereditary.

FLAGS

THE oldest of existing flags is that of Denmark—the Danebrog, which was certainly adopted in the thirteenth century. Tradition says that in A. D. 1219, during a combat with the heathen Esthonians, the white cross of the Danish flag appeared in the sky. It was adopted as a national emblem, and an order of knighthood founded, which, under much-changed conditions, still exists (the Order of the Danebrog). The earliest banners were ecclesiastical. The *oriflamme* of France was the flame-colored banner of the Abbey of St. Denis, which was carried before the army as a sacred sign (A. D. 630). The banner of England, St. George's cross (*argent*, a cross *gules*), had a religious origin also.

SEALS

PHARAOH gave his seal to Joseph (Gen. xli. 42), and Darius sealed the den of lions with his own signet (Dan. vi. 17). The seal of Haggai, son of Shebaniah (B. C. 700), has come down to us, and copies of it can be bought for a trifle.

The seals of monarchs and great nobles prove that during the twelfth century they bore, as personal devices, true armorial bearings. It was not until the return of Richard the Lion-heart from Palestine (1194) that the three lions passant gardant became fixed as the arms of England (Fig. 78). Louis le Jeune of France seals with a fleur-de-lis in 1180. During the Third Crusade (1189) armorial bearings were common, as they had been proved to be useful by experience in war. The English soldiers were distinguished by a white cross sewed to their surcoats; the French bore a red, and the Flemings a green, cross.

The nobles charged their shields with such
personal devices as pleased their fancy, or
as recalled the object of their mission. The
lion, the eagle, the cross, the scallop-shell
of the pilgrim, etc., became common. The
dragon, the wivern (emblem of the Vandals), Saracens' heads, etc., bespeak an
Eastern origin. The double-headed eagle
of the Holy Roman Empire was adopted
from an Asiatic device.

The early ecclesiastical seals were impressed in the form of an elongated pointed
oval,—the shape of a fish,—in allusion to
the Greek initials of the sentence, *Jesus
Christ, the Son of God, the Saviour*—ΙΧΘΥΣ.
As the early universities were ecclesiastical corporations, the seals of colleges often
take this form (see Johns Hopkins University,[1] Fig. 116). The seals of bishops
are, in general, of this form also.

[1] The very beautiful seal of the Johns Hopkins University is reproduced here as a model of what such devices
should be. In the design for the seal, symbols of learning have been added (in the chief) to the well-known
arms of Maryland, which are those of Lord Baltimore
(Cecil Calvert), the first proprietor (1649). The Calvert
arms (in the quarters I and III) are "paly of six, *or* and
sable, a bend dexter counterchanged." Quarters II and

ARMS

ARMS were granted by the greater nobles to the Crusaders for gallant deeds, or they were assumed at will. They were at first merely individual cognizances, but they became hereditary about the end of the thirteenth century. A victorious knight had the privilege of assuming the arms of his vanquished enemy. The Carys of Carisbrook in Virginia bear the arms (*argent,* on a bend *sable,* three roses of the field) which their ancestor, in the reign of Henry V, assumed from those of a Spanish knight whom he overcame in a trial of arms. The three feathers of the crest of the Prince of Wales were once the badge of the King of Bohemia, which, with his motto, *Ich dien,* were assumed by Edward, Prince of Wales,

IV are for Crossland (derived by Lord Baltimore from his grandmother, Alicia Crossland, an heiress), namely, "quarterly *argent* and *gules,* a cross flory counterchanged." The chief is *azure,* and it bears a terrestrial globe *or* between two open books *argent.* The whole seal presents an heraldic picture of a university devoted to science (signified by the globe) and literature (the open books), situated in the State of Maryland.

after the battle of Cressy, where the king was among the slain. The very earliest Crusaders did not bear arms. The shields of the French knights at Constantinople, about 1100, are described by Anna Comnena as polished and plain.

The Bayeux tapestry, tradition says, was embroidered by Matilda, wife of William the Conqueror. At all events, it represents the invasion of England by the Normans, and contains the figures of more than six hundred men, with horses, ships, banners, etc., all worked in colors, with minute attention to detail. Experts are agreed that true armorial bearings are not found in this work, which must have been subsequent to 1066. It was not until the last part of the twelfth century that arms came into general use. No coins bear arms until the thirteenth century. The latest researches indicate that armorial bearings originated about the year 1150. Heraldic seals dated 1157, 1159, 1163, etc., are still extant in Germany.

It is reported that the tomb of Varmond, in the Church of St. Emmeran at Ratisbon, bears a shield parted *per pale*, charged with

a lion over all, and the date MX. It is
likely that the carving was done long afterward in this case, as in many others. The
earliest Pope of Rome who can be proved
to have borne arms is said to have been
Boniface VIII (1294–1303), though arms
are ascribed to nearly all the popes since
Lucius II (1144). The seal of Philip, Count
of Flanders (1164), bears a lion rampant,
which is still the cognizance of Flanders;
and this is one of the very earliest examples of an heraldic device. It is to be
noted that a seal, whose impression was
necessarily contemporaneous with the document to which it was attached, is evidence
of the first importance. Coats of arms can
be cut upon monuments and tombs at any
time, and brasses set up whenever their
evidence is wanted.

[1] For many years the Viscounts MacDuff claimed descent from the ancient Earls of Fife; and to substantiate
the claim an ancient monument (belonging to another
family) was removed to the Duff mausoleum, and the date
altered so as to read (in Arabic numerals!) 1404. A
family of Deardens constructed in Rochdale Church a
complete family chapel, with effigies, slabs, brasses, etc.,
all recording the lives and deaths of a line of sham ancestors, no one of whom ever existed! The lions of England
cut on the monument of William the Conqueror at Caen,

Experts in heraldry are often asked to "explain the meaning" of heraldic charges. Is *gules* a noble color? Does the lion signify generous courage? Does *azure* denote justice, loyalty? *argent*, purity? *or*, force, constancy, riches? Is *sable* a sign of grief? etc. The earliest arms were assumed by individuals at will, or granted for specific deeds; and in such cases there may once have been a special meaning to the shield. Retainers were granted arms resembling those of their overlord. The branches of a family differenced their coats with different tinctures, etc. Many new coats were granted to new men. In most cases there was little "meaning" to the arms; and where there was a significance, it was (usually) soon lost sight of. For example, the arms of Arnold Linden, Comte d'Archot, were *or*, three fleurs-de-lis *sable;* and these arms descended to his eldest son. The second son assumed for arms, *gules*, three fleurs-de-lis *argent;* the third son, *argent*, three fleurs-de-lis *gules;* the fourth son, *argent*, three fleurs-de-lis *sable ;* the fifth son,

in 1642, were never borne by him. Seals impressed on documents cannot be so readily counterfeited.

gules, three fleurs-de-lis *or*. If there were any special significance to the tinctures of the original arms, it was quickly lost in those of the sons. In other families totally different devices were employed by the various branches.

In some cases the arms are rebus-like, and spell the name: as the swallows (*hirondelles*) in the arms of Arundel; the three towers (*tours*) in the arms of Tours; the golden lion in the arms of Lyons; the column in the shield of Colonna; the hen (*Henne*) on a mount (*berg*) for Henneberg; etc. Here we may say the arms have a meaning. The Abbey of St. Denis has among its relics one of the passion nails of the cross; and its shield is charged with a passion nail, in allusion to this precious possession. But in general it may safely be said that coats of arms have now no " meaning," in the usual sense of the term.

As Americans have no central office (like the Heralds' College in England) which has authority over the granting and bearing of arms, and as our governments take no official notice of them (except when they are borne as seals or trade-marks), it is impossible to lay down any rules in their regard that shall be really authoritative. Good taste and good usage must govern us here as elsewhere.

In England, France, Germany, Austria (and in the United States), there is no legal obstacle to the assumption of armorial bearings by any individual or corporation. Any individual has the right to assume and to bear a coat of arms. In most countries those who make use of arms (on seals, carriages, etc.) are subject to an annual tax; and in Germany, etc., the law expressly forbids any individual to bear a coat of arms belonging to another person.[1] The annual tax, and the law protecting each person in the possession of his own coat,

---

[1] The following is a translation of a part of a letter received from the editor of the "German Herald":

"It is lawful for every citizen to assume a coat of arms. He may either bear a coat used by his ancestors, or he may assume and use a coat according to his own pleasure. It is, however, forbidden to assume a coat which is already in use by another family. A register of arms is kept by the Heraldic Society of Berlin (Schillstrasse No. 3), in which arms are entered without cost."

The same rule obtains in Austria and in most countries of the Continent. If heraldry is to be a live science some such provision must be adopted. Otherwise it becomes

serve to regulate the whole matter;[1] and the tax is a very proper means of raising revenue.

The seals of corporations and the trade-marks of individuals may be registered, and governments take measures to insure their exclusive use by those to whom they appertain. Armorial bearings were always strictly regulated in France, and during the reign of Louis XIV they were subject to a tax of twenty livres—or forty if they contained fleurs-de-lis. The Revolution in 1790 swept away arms; but they were again revived under Napoleon, whose heralds devised new charges,—pyramids, etc.,— that recalled his own wars, and not those of the Crusades.

The Heralds' College was established in England in 1483. Its business was to register grants of arms, and to see that such distinctions were not borne illegally. From

of antiquarian interest only. It is a practical fact that arms continue to be used in democratic countries as well as in monarchies. It is therefore only rational to recognize and to reduce to some kind of orderly rule proceedings that cannot be ignored or prevented.

[1] The annual tax in England is one guinea, or two guineas if the arms are borne on carriages.

1528 to 1704 its officials made periodic visitations to the various counties, registering genealogies, etc. It is still in existence, though shorn of much of its power. Arms are still granted by the college to any applicant for a moderate fee (ten pounds).

The Montjoie *roi d'armes* of France dates from the thirteenth century; and the office of Lyon king-at-arms of Scotland was established before 1371. The name "herald" first occurs in 1152 in the imperial constitutions of Frederick Barbarossa, though the office is as old as warfare. Heralds were the spokesmen for all the messages of the king or commanding general.

During the fourteenth, fifteenth, sixteenth, and seventeenth centuries the kings of France ordered various heralds' visitations, because the wrongful assumption of nobility disturbed the incidence of taxes (from many of which nobles were exempt). The most thorough of these visitations was made in 1666–74. It was then laid down as a principle that those nobles who had borne titles and arms continuously since 1560 were to be confirmed in their rights, provided they still held their lands, while those who had alienated their lands were required to prove that they had borne their titles since 1514. In 1714 proofs were required no further back than 1614. A practice dating back one hundred and fifty or one hundred years was sufficient confirmation of a title, therefore, in monarchical France. Those Americans whose ancestors assumed arms in colonial days (as so many did) may be glad to have this precedent to refer to.

The English idea of armorial bearings is that they are given as property to an individual, and from him descend as property to his children and their children. Hence in England there is no such thing as the arms of a *family*, except as the sons, grandsons, etc. (not the brothers), of the grantee constitute *his* particular family. The practice is quite different on the Continent. In theory, every Englishman who bears a coat of arms is noble. *Nobiles sunt qui arma gentilicia antecessorum suorum proferre possunt.* The arms of the *bourgeois* (citizen) are not recognized unless they are registered at the Heralds' College, when he becomes (in strict theory) a petty noble. In Germany, Austria, etc., arms are granted by the emperor to the noble class; but citizens may assume them, and are rather encouraged to do so. When a citizen assumes arms they descend to his children.

If a new coat of arms is to be designed, the following points, among others, should be attended to, and in all cases the advice of an expert should be sought. The shield, helmet, mantling, crest, and the lettering of the motto should all be designed in one style (as of the fourteenth or fifteenth century, etc.), and the models chosen from good examples. The divisions of the shield should be few, the charges simple; but pains should be taken to make the arms in fact new, and not a copy of those of an ancient family. What right has a new man to bear the arms of the Howards or of Hohenlohe? The crest should also be simple, and it may well repeat the colors and the forms of the principal charge of the shield. The helmet should be in profile when the arms are designed for a simple gentleman. The mantling and the wreath should repeat the colors of the shield. In designing the helmet, the artist should re-

member that it was slipped *over* the head,
and that no part of it, therefore, should be
so small that this could not be done. The
helmets of many modern knights, as de-
picted in their coats of arms, could not
be put on even, much less worn. Coats
of arms for cities, corporations, etc., are
usually designed from the *seal* of the city,
etc.

It may be convenient to bring together
a few important dates. *Arms* were first
used by persons about A. D. 1150; on coins
in the thirteenth century. They came into
general use in the thirteenth century, and
at the end of this century they became
hereditary. The oldest grants of arms (in
Germany) date from 1401. *Patents of
nobility* were granted by the German emperors in the second half of the fourteenth
century; in France as early as 1270. Some
cities had *seals* in the twelfth century, and
arms in the middle of the fourteenth.
Crests began to come into use (in England)
about 1300, and soon became general.
Mantlings first appeared (in England) with
Richard I (1189–99), and they were in general use in the fourteenth century. *Sup-*

2

porters were used from about 1300. *Badges* were worn in England before 1400.

HERALDRY IN DIFFERENT COUNTRIES

THE origin of heraldry must be referred to the Crusaders, who brought its customs with them on their return to their native countries. In each country the art has had a different development, so that English, French, and German heraldry have distinctive characters. In all countries the essentials are the same, and in each one heraldry has passed through three distinct and well-marked periods.

In the first period (1150 to about 1200) the shield alone bore the arms. There were no crests. In the second period (1200 to about 1500) the armorial bearings of the warrior displayed the actual shield, helmet, crest, which were worn by him in battle. This is the best period of heraldry, naturally. Fig. 64 (after Albrecht Dürer) may be taken as an example of it.

As the implements of war were perfected, and especially as the use of gunpowder became general and effective, the armor of the knight was modified or laid aside. The third period, that is, modern heraldry, commenced here. Since that epoch heraldry has become a conventionalized art, and its usefulness has been manifested in new directions. A lively picture of the conditions of warfare after the introduction of gunpowder may be had by conceiving the dismay and amazement of the incas of Peru when opposed by the firearms of the conquistadors. An entirely new conception of military skill and valor came in with the harquebus and musket (1575). Gunpowder was the great leveler of the sixteenth century, as steam and electricity have been of the nineteenth.

It may serve to throw light on the development of heraldry in different countries if we compare it with architecture—with Gothic architecture, for example. We have Gothic art exhibited in England, in France, in Germany, but in each country it has developed individual peculiarities. Just as the façade of the cathedral at Rouen is distinctively in the French style, just as that of York is distinctively English, so the style of a French or English coat of

arms is felt by one versed in such matters;
and a sort of pleasure, akin to that derived
from good architecture, is to be had from
an armorial achievement which is well and
suitably composed. No one can mistake
a collection of Russian coats of arms for
French or English. Their national char-
acter is entirely obvious.

In a general way it may be said that German heraldry best represents the spirit of
the middle ages, though a collection of German coats seems to an English herald to lack
somewhat in imagination and variety. The
partitions of the German shield are simple,
colors and metals are well disposed, and the
charges are few. The crests are often elaborate and seem heavy. English and French
heraldry are much alike, though there are
characteristic differences. The use of marks
of cadency in France and England (to distinguish the eldest, the second, the third
son, etc.), and of helmets appropriate to
each rank, are consequences of the law of
primogeniture which prevailed in both
these countries. The eldest son must
needs have his privileges marked and
guarded. *Azure* (the royal color of the

Bourbons) predominates in French shields; *vert* in those of Holland (why?); *gules* (the national color) in those of Poland. The *ermine*, so frequently occurring in English coats of arms, is doubtless a reminiscence of the arms of Brittany (whose shield was *ermine*). Italian heraldry has a style all its own. Italian shields have a special shape also. The symbol of the party of the Guelfs (a chief *azure*, with fleurs-de-lis) and of that of the Ghibellines (the eagle-displayed of the empire) are very common. Spanish and Portuguese heraldry have been much influenced by that of France, though their national styles are plainly marked. The fields are frequently parted in three pieces, and the charges are numerous and confused. Danish heraldry resembles that of France and England, except that rebus arms (*armes parlantes*), which spell the name of the bearer, are more common. Arms in Russia have a well-marked style also. Japan was for centuries under the régime of a feudal system, and an elaborate emblematic armorial was there developed, which is in use to-day. Every noble Japanese family has its emblem, which is emblazoned on the dress and weapons.

The principal sources from which the history of heraldry can be derived are seals, coins, monuments, tombs, patents of nobility, grants of land or arms, the visitations and other records of the heralds, records of tournaments, rolls of arms, portraits (which often bear the arms of the sitter), coats of arms carved on the exterior of buildings or in their interior decorations, woven in tapestries, etc. Almost every large library in the United States has a section devoted to works on heraldry and genealogy, and those who have read this little book will find it a good introduction to further explorations in this interesting field. Excellent articles on heraldry are to be found in many books of reference, and the reader may well consult these after he has mastered the principles here set forth. Perhaps the best of them within the reach of everybody are to be found in the Encyclopædia Britannica, in Johnson's Encyclopedia, and (under various heads) in the Century Dictionary. Many of the excellent cuts of this book are taken from the latter work. In the cyclopedia of Chambers (which gives great prominence to Scottish matters) the reader will do well to consult the articles on the chief Scottish families, as Argyle, Bruce, Douglas, Lindsay, Mar, Stewart, etc. The Almanach de Gotha gives the genealogy, etc., of the princely houses of Europe. There are similar works relating to the counts, the barons, etc.

HERALDRY IN ARCHITECTURE

GOTHIC architecture can scarcely be appreciated in its details without a considerable knowledge of heraldry. It was a universal custom to display the coat of arms on buildings, tombs, monuments, windows, etc. The same custom is wide-spread in the United States, where the seals of the States and departments are to be found on many public buildings. The monuments erected at Gettysburg display the State seals, the badges of army-corps, etc., in a very instructive fashion.

The new University Club in New York is to display the arms of American colleges on its façade. The new Library of Con-

gress, in Washington, contains (in the read-
ing-room) the arms of the States of the
Union in colored glass.

It is worth while to have some knowledge
of the pictorial language of heraldry in
order to derive the great pleasure which
comes through such a familiarity. An heraldic device, displayed in the right place
and in the right way, produces precisely the
kind of pleasure which a scholar feels from
an apposite quotation.[1]

HERALDRY IN LITERATURE AND HISTORY

IF history is to be written at first hand,
original documents must be consulted, and
these cannot be properly understood without a knowledge of heraldry, which enables
one to decipher the seals that they bear

[1] For instance, the seal of Harvard College on the
eighteenth-century gateways to its grounds; the Mapes
memorial gateway at the new Columbia University in
New York. But, on the other hand, what are these *"eagles
with wings displayed checky"* doing in front of the Boston
Public Library? They are a part of the arms of a noble
Roman family. They are certainly decorative; but they
are as appropriate in that place as a door-plate "Beau-
champs" would be on Governor Winthrop's mansion—no
more, no less.

and by which they are authenticated. This is not only true of England and Europe, but also of the colonial period in America. All colonial papers were sealed by either public or private signets, and the seal employed will often fix the date of the document.

As heraldry was a part of daily life up to very recent times, and a most essential part from 1200 to 1700, it is naturally reflected in history and throughout literature. Fully to understand what one reads, these allusions must not be missed for want of a little study. The history of trade is illustrated by the arms of the powerful London companies (gilds), which received their charters from 1327 onward; and the seals of the Oxford and Cambridge colleges constitute a most interesting chapter in the history of learned foundations.

The connection of families can often be traced by their arms and in no other way; as Guillim says, in his "Heraldry": "The Shaws are known to be McIntoshes by their arms." The relation of the early American emigrants to the English (and Dutch, French, etc.) families from whom they descend is often to be fixed by arms or crests engraved on silver plate, or by signet-rings, etc. Comparatively little use was made of arms in America during the century 1620–1720. It was a period of stress, and distinctions of rank were more or less forgotten. With acquired wealth came leisure and a general desire to connect one's self with the mother-country. From 1700 onward more attention was paid to such matters, and arms were quite generally borne by those who inherited them, or were assumed by others who had acquired fortune. The cemeteries of Boston, New York, Newport, Philadelphia, Annapolis, Richmond, etc., contain many gravestones engraved with armorial bearings. A few date from the seventeenth century; most are later than 1720.

It is not possible to read the plays of Shakspere, the poems of Chaucer, Spenser, Tasso, Ariosto, Scott, Tennyson, and others, with full understanding without some knowledge of heraldic rules and language.

Awake, awake, English nobility! Cropped are the flower-de-luces in your arms! of England's coat one half is cut away (SHAKSPERE, *Henry VI*, Part 1, act i, sc. 1),

refers to the lilies of France, which Edward III had quartered with the lions of England.

> Where is proud Scotland's royal shield,
> The ruddy lion ramped in gold
>   (SCOTT, *Marmion*, Canto IV),

is one of the hundreds of allusions in Sir Walter Scott's poems and tales to armorial bearings.

THE COAT OF ARMS

The Shield.—Arms are generally borne upon a shield to signify their military origin. The shape of the shield may be chosen at will, but it is essential, in good heraldic drawing, to have the style of the heraldic achievement harmonious throughout. A shield of the thirteenth century must not be surmounted by a helmet of the sixteenth, nor accompanied by a mantling of the seventeenth. Too little attention is paid by artists to this matter of style. The shield was originally made of wood and covered with leather (on which the arms were stamped) or with parchment (on which they were painted). Metal bands, fessewise, palewise, bendwise,[1] etc., and bosses were used to strengthen the shield; and some of the ordinaries of heraldry have probably been thence derived. A number of ancient shields are still extant—usually in churches in Europe, or in museums. The shield of Heinrich of Hesse (died 1298) is still to be seen in Marburg, for example.

The pointed Norman shields (Figs. 3, 4, 5, 6, 7, 54) are the most graceful in form, and they are well suited to simple blazons. The conventionalized shields (like Fig. 51) are convenient for displaying charges, and are here employed for that reason only; but they are not suitable for seals, illuminated drawings, etc. The proper procedure is to select, from ancient drawings or monuments, the forms for crest, mantling, shield, and charges, and to reproduce them all in one consistent style. The style of any century may be chosen at will. Figs. 106–112 are instructive in this connection, and especially Fig. 64.

The shape of the shield employed is more

_____
[1] That is, horizontal, vertical, inclined.

or less determined by the arrangement of the bearings to be charged upon it, and it is an essential of good design that the charges should fill the entire shield. The *size* of a charge has no relation to its significance. The three lions of Fig. 78 have equal importance.

The shield of a man, a warrior, the head of a house, is, as has been said, a knight's shield, and it is surmounted by his crest. His wife, in English practice, may bear his arms on his shield, but *without* the crest. His daughters may bear their father's arms on a lozenge (◊). The French practice is to blazon the arms of *all* women on lozenge-shaped or oval shields. The arms of nations, of provinces, cities, etc., are borne on a knight's shield. Monasteries, colleges, and the like often employ a pointed oval as a shield (see Fig. 116).

Parts of the Shield. — In describing a shield and its charges, it is always supposed to be borne as in war. That is, the left-hand side in Fig. 1 is called the *dexter* side, the right hand the *sinister*. The upper third of the shield is the *chief*. *E*, in Fig. 2, is the *fesse-point*, *F* the *nombril-point*. Nom-

bril-points are not named in English heraldry, though they are used on the Continent. The whole surface of the shield is
called the *field*. It is necessary for the
reader to pay some attention to the definitions of this section. They give the heraldic
alphabet, as it were, without which the blazon of a shield cannot be read.

Division of the Shield (see Figs. 3, 4, 5, 6,
7).—The shield is seldom all of one color.
It is generally divided into parts. It is
parted *per pale* in Fig. 3; *per fesse* in Fig.
4; quartered in Fig. 5; parted *per bend*
(dexter) in Fig. 6; *per saltire* in Fig. 7. A
shield may be parted *per bend sinister* also.
If it is divided into *any* number of equal
parts with square corners, as six, eight,
twelve, sixteen parts, etc., it is said to be
quarterly of six, eight, etc. The lines of
division may not always be straight lines.
They may be a single smooth curve
(*embowed*), or composed of several curves
(*undé*), or edged like a saw (*indented*), or
like battlements (*embattled*), etc. (see Figs.
8, 9, 10, 11, 12, 13).

Tinctures. — The surface of the shield is
supposed to be covered, wholly or in part,
by either metals, furs, or colors.

The heraldic metals are two: gold, *or;* silver, *argent.* If the shield is emblazoned in colors, these are to be painted yellow and white respectively. They may be represented conventionally in black and white, as in Fig. 18 and Figs. 1, 2, etc. (*i. e.,* a plain shield signifies *argent*).

The principal heraldic colors are:

Red—*gules*   (see Figs. 19 and 23);
Blue—*azure*   (see Figs. 20 and 23);
Black—*sable*   (see Figs. 21 and 23);
Green—*vert*   (see Figs. 22 and 23);
Purple—*purpure* (see Fig. 23).

The latter color seldom occurs in English coats of arms. In French heraldry *vert* is called *sinople*, and flesh-color is called *carnation.* Fig. 23 also shows the conventional method of depicting other colors (rarely used), as *tenné, sanguine,* etc.

Of the heraldic furs, three are most common, viz.:

Ermine (see Fig. 24);
Vair[1]   (see Fig. 25);
Potent (see Fig. 26).

[1] Dr. Edward Everett Hale shrewdly surmises that Cinderella's slippers were of fur=*vair*, and not of glass=*verre.*

Other furs are shown in Figs. 27, 28, 29.
If new coats are to be devised, it is convenient to employ these rarely used furs,
especially as they lend themselves to effective designs.

The shield is wholly covered with these
metals, furs, and colors. Upon it are
"charged" certain devices, which are also
of metals, furs, and colors. A fundamental rule of blazoning is that metal
must not be superposed on metal, nor fur
on fur, nor color on color. A lion *gules*,
for example, must not be charged on a field
azure, nor a lion *argent* on a field *or*.

> Color may be placed on metal or fur.
> Metal "   "   "   " color or fur.
> Fur   "   "   "   " metal or color.

These rules have been universally followed in modern times, especially in England. There are many ancient coats,
however, that do not conform to the
rule. The arms of the kingdom of Jerusalem, for instance, consist of crosses *or*
charged on a field *argent;* the arms of the
Inquisition in Spain were *sable*, a cross
vert. Moreover, when a charge is blazoned

in its *proper* color the rule does not apply. *Azure*, an oak-tree *proper* (*i. e.*, *vert*), is an allowable blazon.

CHARGES

A *charge* is any figure or device placed upon a shield. In the nature of things most shields must be distinguished by charges. The arms of D'Albret were originally a field *gules* without any other thing, says Froissart, until "the French king gave to his cousin-german, Sir Charles d'Albret, for the augmentation of his honor, two quarters of arms of France with flower-de-luces." The arms of Brittany are *ermine* and no more. But only a few shields can be composed with simple tinctures and without charges.

The heralds have divided charges into several classes. It is only necessary here to distinguish two, namely, ordinaries and common charges.

The *ordinaries* are as follows: The *chief*, which occupies the upper third of the field (see Fig. 30). Its diminutive is the *fillet*— one fourth of the chief, and lying at its

3

base. The *pale* is a vertical band, one third
of the width of the shield (see Fig. 14).
The *pallet* is one half of the pale. The
bend (dexter) is as in Fig. 31 when it bears
another charge (as a lion, an eagle, etc.), and
it then is one third the width of the shield
(see Figs. 12 and 51). If it bears no charge
it must be one fifth of this width. It has
several diminutives (see Fig. 33). The *bend
sinister* crosses the shield diagonally from
sinister to dexter. It is *not* the sign of
illegitimate birth. The *baton* is one fourth
the width of the *bend*. It is *couped* (cut off)
at its extremities, and is often used to mark
illegitimacy. The cadets of the house of
Bourbon bore the baton; the illegitimate
sons the baton sinister (Fig. 34).

The *fesse* (Fig. 35) is one third the width
of the shield, and the *bar* (Fig. 35 bis), is
one fifth of this width. (The bar is borne in
groups of two, three, etc. The *fesse* is fixed
in position, while bars may be placed any-
where in the field. A "bar sinister" is an
impossible charge.) For various forms of
the fesse see Figs. 8, 9, 10, 11. The *chevron*
(Fig. 36) is formed of two bars conjoined
(see also Figs. 56 and 57). A *chevronel* is

a small chevron of half-width. In continental heraldry the bend, fesse, and chevron
are often arched or bowed (as in the arms
of Saxony, for example). The *saltire* is a
St. Andrew's cross; its form is shown in
Fig. 37. The cross of St. Patrick, Ireland,
is *argent*, a saltire *gules;* the cross of St.
Andrew, Scotland, is *azure*, a saltire *argent*.

The Cross (see Fig. 38, which is the cross of
St. George, England, *argent*, a cross *gules*).
—There are very many forms of the cross.
When no special designation is given the
form of Fig. 38 is implied. Drawings of many
of the forms are given in Figs. 39, 40, 41, 42,
43, 44, 45, and 46. In Fig. 46 the *Latin
cross* (2) has its lower limb the longer. The
Greek cross is as in No. 7. The *patriarchal
cross* (5) is a cross with a short bar across
its upper limb. The *cross of St. Anthony*
(3) is like the Greek letter *tau*. The *cross
potent* (Jerusalem cross) is shown in No. 13.
The *Maltese cross* (10) (so called because it
was the cognizance of the Knights of Malta)
is well known. The *cross crosslet* (Fig. 39)
is a cross each of whose limbs is traversed
by a short bar. If the lower limb of a cross
is sharpened as if to fix it in the ground,

it is described as *fitché*. Such crosses were set up by the Crusaders in their devotions (see Fig. 45). Crosses and saltires may be " voided," as in Fig. 37 bis.

The *quarter* is, as the name implies, one fourth of the field (see Figs. 5, 51, 52, 57). The *canton* is a little quarter occupying one third of the chief, usually on the dexter side (see Fig. 47). The *gyron* is half of a quarter, bisected bendwise (see Fig. 48, where the whole field is gyronny). The gyron is said to have originated in Spanish heraldry. The *bordure* is one fifth of the width of the shield (see Fig. 49). It is frequently added to a coat of arms, especially on the Continent, to distinguish an offshoot of a family from the original stock; or, as frequently, in Spain, as an augmentation of honor. The *tressure* is one fourth of the bordure. In the arms of Scotland it is borne double, and *fleury-counter-fleury*, *i. e.*, with eight fleurs-de-lis issuing from each tressure (Fig. 50). These fleurs-de-lis are said to allude to the early alliances of Scotland with France.

The *inescutcheon* is a small shield borne on the center of the field (Fig. 52). *Bezants* are small *roundels* of *or* (see Fig. 16 for roundels).

When a shield consists of more than one tincture, the dividing-lines are described, as to their direction, as in the titles to Figs. 3, 4, 5, 6, 7, 15, 16, 17, 61, 62, 63. Fig. 15 is blazoned paly of six, because the lines divide the shield into six parts and lie in the direction of the pale. Fig. 61 is blazoned barry of six, etc. A field *checky* is divided like a chess-board (Fig. 62). The Stewarts bear a fesse checky. They were at first hereditary stewards of the Scottish kings; and the checkered board was used in making up accounts, it is said.

The foregoing gives an account of the *ordinaries* and most of the *subordinaries*. The reader should consult the titles to the various figures in the plates at the end of this book. See especially Figs. 58, 59, 60. We have now to consider what figures may be charged upon the field, or upon any one of the ordinaries.

Common Charges.—Any device may be charged upon the field,—animals, birds, letters of the alphabet, weapons, etc.,—and all such devices, except the *ordinaries* just

described, are called "common charges."
Each of these devices may be represented
in its native tints (when it is called *proper*),
or it may be displayed in any one of the
heraldic metals, furs, or colors. A lion
vert would be a zoölogical curiosity, but it
is a perfectly correct heraldic charge. The
forms of heraldic animals, etc., are highly
conventionalized also. For instance, an
heraldic lion is all mouth and paws; the
features which represent his ferocity and
strength are purposely exaggerated. A conventional heraldic style has been evolved in
the course of centuries, which is not without its excellences, and which gives pleasure to the expert. Fig. 64 is an admirable
example of medieval heraldic design (in
Germany), by Albrecht Dürer. It is a
combination of medieval design with Re-
naissance forms.

Heraldic animals are described as to their
position in technical terms, as *rampant,
sejant,* etc. An examination of the figures
at the end of this book will convey a better notion of the heraldic postures than
verbal descriptions. In German heraldry
it is indifferent in which direction the

charges face. In English they always face
to dexter, as has been said. If the arms of
man and wife are marshaled on two shields,
or on the same shield side by side (see Fig.
65), it is a fixed rule in Germany that the
charges must face toward each other, so
that the arms of the *baron* (dexter half of
the shield) are necessarily *contourné*, while
those of the *femme* (sinister half) face in
their natural direction. All English helmets in profile must also face to the dexter; but it is not so in Germany. This rule
is carried so far that in German heraldic
books it has been customary to make all
the charges and helmets face toward the
inner side of the pages! This would not
be tolerated in English practice. A few of
the more important charges will be named.
Heraldic terms not given here may be found
in the Century Dictionary.

The *lion* (see Figs. 33, 55, 67, 68, 69, 70,
71, 72, 73, 74, 75, 76, 77, and 78). The lion
was for several centuries the charge most
frequently used. In a roll of the time of
Edward II the arms of 918 bannerets are
given. Lions occur in 225 coats; and
eagles, a very frequent charge, in 43. It

has been the badge (cognizance) of England since the time of Henry I (A. D. 1127). Lions may be *statant*[1] (standing), *passant* (walking), *passant gardant* (walking with the full face seen), *rampant* (as in Fig. 33), *salient* (as in Fig. 70), *sejant* (seated), etc. Lions are generally blazoned "armed and langued *gules*," *i. e.*, with claws and tongue (*langue*) *gules*, unless the field is *gules*, in which case the color is usually *azure*.

The *stag* (see Figs. 82, 83, 84, 85, 86). A stag is not said to be *passant*, but *trippant*; not *salient*, but *springing*; not *sejant*, but *lodged*; etc.

The *eagle* (see Figs. 87, 88). The eagle is usually *displayed*, *i. e.*, as in the arms of the United States, Russia, etc. It is single-headed in the arms of the United States, ancient Rome, Germany, etc.; double-headed for Russia,[2] Austria, the Holy Roman Empire,[3] etc. The eagle of Mexico, with the cactus, is derived from Aztec manuscripts.

---

[1] These words are pronounced as they are spelled *in English*, not as in Norman French.

[2] The Czar of Russia assumed the double-headed eagle as a cognizance, in 1470, on his marriage with the niece of the last Byzantine emperor.

[3] The double-headed eagle has been the cognizance

The *boar* (see Fig. 17).

The *peacock* is said to be "*in his pride*" when the tail is spread.

The *pelican* is said to be "*in her piety*" when in the nest feeding her young with blood from her breast. Other birds are shown in Figs. 89, 90, 91.

The wings of birds, in pairs or single, are very common in the crests of German heraldry. A plume of (three) feathers is the badge of the Prince of Wales. It was assumed from that of the King of Bohemia who was killed at the battle of Cressy (1346), and has since been the cognizance of the princes of Wales. Three *allerions* (eagles without beaks or claws) occur in the arms of Lorraine (*alérion* = *loraine*).

The *martlet* is a swallow with no beak and no feet, and is frequently found in English heraldry (see Fig. 89).

Fish. A fish is *haurient* when it is in *pale* with the head upward. A dolphin (*dauphin*) was the cognizance of the dauphins of France (see Fig. 92). It is usually *embowed* (see also Figs. 93, 94).

since the beginning of the fifteenth century. Before that time the emperor bore the eagle with a single head.

Wild men or *savages* are most frequently met with as supporters.

Parts of the human body (a hand, an arm, etc.) are often used as charges. The heart (of Bruce) appears in the arms of Douglas (Fig. 95).

The *dragon* (see Fig. 79). The dragon is an heraldic charge, either with or without St. George (see the beautiful design on the obverse of the gold sovereigns of the English currency). The *cockatrice* and *wivern* are fabulous beasts of the same nature, and, like the dragon, have heraldic forms all their own (Figs. 80 and 81).

The *sun* usually appears "*in his splendor,*" *i. e.*, front face, or with rays (as in the seal of Bowdoin College, for example) (Fig. 53).

The *moon* is usually either *crescent* (Fig. 96) (a new moon with the horns pointing upward), or *increscent* (horns to dexter), or *decrescent* (horns to sinister). The three crescents interlaced of Fig. 97 is a very old design of religious origin.

Stars have six wavy points (see Fig. 98). A five-pointed star is heraldically a *mullet*. The *mullet* as a charge is often *pierced, i. e.,* with a hole in the center, through which the tincture of the field shows.

Trees. The oak is most common, or the roots and branches. Trees appear in crests more frequently than as charges.

The *fleur-de-luce* (see Fig. 54). "France ancient" bore *azure* sprinkled with (many) lilies *or*, as in Fig. 54. "France modern" bore *azure*, with three lilies only, arranged "two and one," *i. e.*, with two lilies in chief and one in base. The fleurs-de-lis have figured in the arms of France since Louis VII (1179). Charles V (1364) first reduced their number to three. They were early introduced into English heraldry, and occur twenty times in the roll of Edward II. Whatever may have been the origin of the charge now called fleur-de-lis, it is certain that it was not originally designed to represent a lily. It is a very old emblem. The Empress Theodora (A. D. 527), for instance, bears one in her crown.

The *rose.* The rose *gules* was the badge of the house of Lancaster, the rose *argent* of the house of York. A rose quarterly *argent* and *gules* was the badge of Henry VII, and is known as the Tudor rose.

The *thistle* is the emblem of Scotland.

The *shamrock* (quatrefoil) is the emblem of Ireland.

Several of the States of the Union have formally adopted a flower as an emblem, as follows: *Alabama*, the goldenrod; *California*, the yellow poppy; *Colorado*, the columbine; *Delaware*, the peach-blossom; *Idaho*, the syringa; *Maine*, the pine-cone and tassel; *Minnesota*, the cypripedium; *Montana*, the bitter-root; *Nebraska*, the goldenrod; *New York*, the rose; *Oklahoma*, the mistletoe; *Oregon*, the goldenrod; *Utah*, the sego-lily; *Vermont*, the red clover; *Rhode Island* and *Wisconsin*, the maple-tree.

A *garb* (or *gerbe*) is a sheaf of wheat.

A *mount vert* (usually in the base of a shield) is a green mound of earth out of which other charges rise (as in the beautiful and appropriate seal of the United States Department of Agriculture) (see Fig. 118).

The *broad-arrow* is often found as a charge. The master-general of the ordnance (1693) used this charge, which occurred in his coat of arms, to mark cannon, etc. Ever since that day it has been employed as a mark for government stores in general at all British stations, and it is as well known as the lions of England.

The *castle* appears in the arms of Castile (*gules*, a castle *or*).

The *ladder* is found in Galileo's arms and in the arms of the Scaligers of Verona.

The *spear*. The arms granted to Shakspere's father were *or*, on a bend *sable*, a tilting-spear of the field (*i. e., or*).

The *sword*. The arms granted to Joan of Arc were *azure*, a sword in pale, point upward, supporting a royal crown, between two fleurs-de-lis *or* (Fig. 32 shows a sword in bend).

When there is more than one charge on a shield, it is necessary to specify the position of each one. Three charges of one kind (in English heraldry) are always arranged "two and one" unless otherwise specified. In continental heraldry the arrangement is always described.

Cadency.—The arms of a father descend, of right, to all his sons, each of whom may in turn become the head of a family. In early times the "differences" employed to mark the various branches were obtained by the use of bordures, by changing the colors of the coat, etc. English practice prescribes the following rules, which have not been strictly followed, however: The eldest son bears the paternal arms, "differenced" by a *label*, *i. e.*, by a sign like the device in chief of Fig. 102. Here the father's arms would be *or*, and the eldest son's coat would be *or*, a label of three points *argent*. The second son differences *his* coat by a *crescent* (Fig. 96), the third son by a *mullet* (a five-pointed star), the fourth by a *martlet* (Fig. 89), etc. The grandsons (during the life of their grandfather) difference their coats in the same manner. The second son of the eldest son would place a crescent upon his father's label, or "mark of cadency."

Englishmen entitled to bear arms brought coats so differenced to America; and marks of cadency—labels, crescents, etc.—still remain on many American coats, and have, in fact, now become a part of the arms. They were not removed at the death of the parent, as they should have been. The arms of daughters are not differenced in this manner, as they are incapable of founding a family. So long as they are unmarried their arms are the same as those of their father. If his arms are differenced, theirs must be, of course. The marks of cadency should be borne on the crest and on the supporters, as well as on the arms, in English heraldry, according to rule.

As we have seen, the shield may be divided in different ways by a few partition-lines. The different parts may be of different tinctures, and a comparatively small number of charges may be superposed on the shield in differing positions. These are the elements from which armorial bearings are built up, and they lend themselves to a great variety of relatively simple combinations. It has been estimated that there are at least two hundred thousand different coats of arms known to-day.[1]

It is by no means difficult to compose an entirely new coat that shall be simple and yet entirely distinct from any coat now in use.

While the right of bearing arms was

[1] The "Armorial Général" of M. Riestap (1861) alone contains the coats of more than sixty thousand families.

formerly confined to the class of nobles,
merchants were permitted to adopt distinctive devices,—*merchants' marks,*—which
were placed upon their merchandise. Such
marks, which are often mere monograms
or letters of the alphabet, are frequently
found in Polish coats of arms as charges.
Of printers' marks, the best known is that
of Aldus—the dolphin and the anchor.
In modern times we find ancestral arms
put to practical use as trade-marks. The
Montebello champagne is marked with the
arms granted by Napoleon to Marshal
Lannes (*vert,* a naked sword in pale), and
there are many like instances.

HELMETS

ABOVE the shield, and solidly resting
upon it, is the helmet. It is full-faced
with bars, for kings, princes, and the
higher nobility; full-faced, open, for baronets and knights; in profile, closed, for es-
quires and gentlemen—in English practice,
and also in French. These rules do not
apply in Germany. Upon the helmet rests
the wreath, a twisted band (six twists) of
two tinctures. The principal metal of the

arms occupies the first, third, and fifth twists (counting from the dexter), and the principal color occupies the other twists. For different forms of helmets see Figs. 106, 107, 108, 109, 110, 111, 119, and 64.

CRESTS

CRESTS came into general use in the thirteenth century, and are an essential part of the arms. In German practice they often repeat the charges on the shield, and are very elaborate and of exaggerated size —very much larger than the shield, in many cases. The arms of the dukes of Mecklenburg are *or*, a bull's head *sable*, crowned *gules*. Their crest is a fan *or* and *gules*, supporting a peacock's tail, and between the latter and the fan the shield is repeated. This crest, with its helmet, must necessarily be drawn very much larger than the shield. Many German crests bear horns in pairs, with or without additions. Wings in pairs occur very frequently in German heraldry as crests. In English practice there is seldom a relation between the crest and the charges of the shield.

4

The crest is in theory a badge, to be assumed at will by an individual. In practice the crest, like the arms, usually remains the same from father to son. In England the crest is frequently displayed over a wreath of the colors; in Germany it is never separated from the helmet, on which it must rest solidly. German heralds make merry over our English crests floating in the air. In Germany all crests face as the helmet faces. If this is in face, so must be the crest; if in profile, the crest must also be in profile. This rule does not obtain in England, though it is the logical practice (see Fig. 55, however, where it is carried out; and compare Fig. 71). The German helmet may be borne full face or in profile, according to fancy. In England (and in France) each rank has its appropriate helmet. Moreover, a quartered coat (*i. e.*, quarterings of various coats derived from different families) in Germany always has the right to at least two helmets and crests, though they are not always borne. In England it is not common to display more than a single helmet and crest, even when the right exists.

CROWNS AND CORONETS

THE helmet is often crowned, or the crown may appear without the helmet. Fig. 105 represents various crowns and coronets, such as are engraved on the visiting-cards of noblemen in continental countries. The *chapeau* (a red cap turned up *ermine*), the miter, the bishop's hat, etc., take the place of the helmet in appropriate cases.

SUPPORTERS

IN English heraldry supporters are used only for the nobility and for a very few other persons. No woman (except the Queen and peeresses) is authorized to bear her coat of arms with supporters. In Germany the practice is entirely different, and good authorities hold that any person is free to assume supporters at will. Usually the supporters have no relation to the charges of the shield (the savages of Prussia, the angels of ancient France, the griffins of Austria, etc.); but occasionally there is such a relation (the *bears* of *Orsini*, the *monks* of *Monaco*, etc.).

BADGES

BADGES were borne by nobles at least as early as coats of arms, and they continued in common use in England down to the times of Queen Elizabeth. The *planta genista* (broom) of the Plantagenets, the roses of York (white) and Lancaster (red), the bear and ragged staff of Earl Warwick, are well known:

> The rampant bear chained to a ragged staff
> This day I'll wear aloft my burgonet
> (SHAKSPERE, *Henry VI*, Part II, act v, sc. 1).

The Scottish clans still employ their badges of heather (Buccleugh), ivy (Gordon), pine (MacGregor), thistle (Stewart), etc., to which their chiefs (only) add two eagle's feathers. Badges are cognizances —the marks by which individuals are distinguished.

MOTTOS

THE motto was anciently the *cri-de-guerre* (the war-cry) as well as the personal motto of the noble. Froissart speaks of "the cry, arms, and name" as if this were the order of their importance; and it is true that war-cries were not permitted to the lesser nobles. Again, it is probable that the arms did in fact precede the family name in many cases. The device in the shield of the noble gave the name to the family in some instances. The swallow (*hirondelle*) in the arms of Arundel was the origin of the family name. The family name or motto is frequently implied in the arms or crest (*armes parlantes*). Thus Sir Thomas Lucy, Shakspere's enemy, bore *lucies* (a fish, the pike); the Spurrs bear spur-rowels; Wolff von Wolffthal (Germany) a wolf in arms and crest; the dauphins of France a dolphin (*dauphin*); etc. Hereditary surnames were not adopted until the thirteenth, and were not common till the fourteenth, century. The French *de* (De la Roche, for example) shows that many surnames arose from the name of a property, etc. There were few Americans bearing *three* names before 1770.

In old German heraldry mottos were not employed. Bismarck's motto, *In Trinitate*

Robur, is not hereditary. It was assumed by the present prince when he received the decoration of the Danebrog from the King of Denmark. *Dieu et mon droit*, is the motto of England; *Gott mit uns*, of Prussia; *Plus ultra*, of Spain; *E pluribus unum*, of the United States; etc. F. E. R. T. (the device of the house of Savoy) stands for *Fortitudo ejus Rhodum tenuit*. The device of the house of Austria—the five vowels —may be interpreted, *Austria Est Imperare Orbi Universo;* etc. The war-cry of the Templars was *Beauséant*, in allusion to their black-and-white flag. *Beauséant* is Old French for a black-and-white charger.

The motto of the coat of arms may be a purely personal one as well as the war-cry. Mme. de Genlis, speaking of personal mottos, well says: "Chaque personne, par sa devise, révèle un petit secret, ou prend une sorte d'engagement." A few mottos may be here set down as examples.

Aberdeen: *Bon Accord* (A. D. 1308).
The French Academy: *À l'immortalité.*
Beauharnais: *Autre ne sers.*
Sara Bernhardt: *Quand même.*
Douglas: *Jamais arrière.*

Erasmus (with a figure of the god Terminus): *Credo nulli.*

Louis XIV (with a sun in splendor [1]): *Nec pluribus impar.*

Mistral the poet (with a locust): *Le soleil me fait chanter.*

Montaigne: *Sais-je ?*

Peter the Great, in Holland, sealed with a signet on which the device was a carpenter's apprentice and the motto: *Mon rang est celui d'un écolier, et j'ai besoin de maîtres.*

Rohan: *Plaisance!*

Mme. de Sévigné (with a swallow): *Le froid me chasse.*

Voltaire: *Au fait.*

KNOTS

KNOTS are a kind of personal badge (see Fig. 101, which gives the principal forms of heraldic knots).

BLAZONING

BLAZONING [2] a coat of arms means its accurate description in heraldic terms,

---

[1] Charles V of France used the same device, according to Froissart.

[2] Blazon (blazonry) is the doctrine according to which arms are described and marshaled. The word is probably derived from the German *blasen*, to blow, in allusion

so that it can be understood or drawn out from the description. The language of the herald is technical and brief, and its use cannot be learned except by practice on many examples. Only the barest outline of the art can be given here. In the first place, the description (the blazon) must be brief, and all tautology must be avoided. Each charge must be mentioned in the strict order of its importance (in the order of its nearness to the surface of the shield, for example). The first mention of a color (or metal) must give its name, as *gules*, *azure*, etc., and this name must not be repeated. If it is necessary to refer to the color again, it is called "the first," "the second," etc. Thus a silver field with a green fesse, charged with two green crosses above the fesse and one below it, and bearing on the fesse itself three silver stars of five points, would be blazoned: *argent*, a fesse *vert* between three crosses of the second, as many mullets of the first. This blazon, and others like it, becomes very

to the trumpets of the heralds at tournaments, where the name, arms, and lineage of the contending knights were proclaimed.

plain when we recollect the fundamental rule that color must not be charged on color, nor metal on metal. The silver mullets *must* be on the fesse. If the student will carefully read the titles to the figures given in this book (especially Figs. 16, 17, 56, 57, 64, etc.) he will obtain some insight into the rules of blazon.

MARSHALING

A COAT OF ARMS is hereditary. Every son inherits the paternal coat. If there are no sons, all the daughters (heiresses) inherit it, and can transmit it to their children. When one marries the arms go with the alliance. The husband has the right to "marshal" her coat with his, and their children inherit the new quartered coat. The marshaling of such complex coats has been performed in various ways at different epochs. Anciently the husband's coat was cut in two per pale (dimidiated), and its dexter half formed the dexter half of the new shield (A, Fig. 3), while the sinister half (B in the same figure) was formed of the sinister half of the heiress's coat. This arrangement was very

unsatisfactory, for obvious reasons. Parts
of three lions of the husband's coat might
be continued by parts of three ships of the
wife's, etc. The next process (about A. D.
1500) was to marshal by impalement. In
Fig. 65, A, is the whole of the husband's coat,
B, the whole of the wife's. The modern
fashion is as follows: The husband bears his
paternal arms (A) on a shield, and over the
shield an inescutcheon (a small shield cen-
trally placed, as in Fig. 52) bearing the arms
(B) of the heiress, his wife. Unless his
wife is in fact an heiress, he may not bear
her arms. The children of such a marriage
bear a quartered coat (see Fig. 5), with the
paternal arms in the first and fourth, the
maternal in the second and third, quarters,
thus $\frac{A\ B}{B\ A}$. Should the issue of such a marriage be an only daughter (heiress), she would
carry the quartered coat to her husband.
During his life he would bear his paternal
arms (C), with his wife's quartered coat on
an inescutcheon; their children would bear
a coat of six quarters, and so on (see Figs.
51, 52, 57, for examples of quartered coats
of arms). Such is the English practice.

The custom in Germany and France (and
also in Scotland) is far more rational.
Every ancestor and ancestress who has a
coat of arms is represented in the quarter-
ing. It would be well to adopt this rule in
America. The coat of the German Empire
contains a quarter for every province. The
arms of Castile and Leon are quarterly, I
and IV Castile (*gules,* a castle *or*), II and III
Leon (*argent,* a lion rampant *gules*), and so on.

In order to give the reader a little needed
practice, the blazons of a few simple coats
of arms are given below. If he will sketch
out for himself the divisions of the various
fields, and indicate the disposition of the
different charges, he will acquire considerable familiarity with the elements of the
subject, and will be prepared to attack
more complex cases.

Angoulême: France ancient (*i. e., azure,*
sprinkled with fleurs-de-lis *or*), a label of
three points *gules.*

Anjou: France modern (*i.e. azure,* three
fleurs-de-lis *or*), a bordure *gules.*

Aragon: paly of ten, *argent* and *gules.*

Arundell of Wardour: *sable,* six swallows *argent,* 3, 2, 1.

Austria: *gules*, a fesse *argent*.

Sir Francis Bacon: *gules*, on a chief *argent*, two mullets pierced *sable* (*i. e.*, two five-pointed black stars with white centers).

Baden: *or*, a bend *gules*.

Brandenburg: *argent*, an eagle displayed *gules*.

Bruce: *or*, a saltire and chief *gules*.

Châteaubriant: *gules*, semé (sprinkled) with fleurs-de-lis *or* (like Fig. 54).

Chaucer: per pale *argent* and *gules*, a bend counterchanged (*i. e.*, the dexter half of the bend is *gules*; the sinister is *argent*). For examples of counterchanging see Figs. 16, 17, and 116.

Croy: *argent*, three bars *gules*.

De Vogüé: *azure*, a game-cock *or*, wattled and armed *gules* (*i. e.*, with red dewlaps and spurs).

Douglas: *argent*, a human heart *gules*, ensigned (*i. e.*, crowned) with a royal crown *proper*, on a chief *azure*, two stars of the first (*i.e.*, *argent*) (see Fig. 95 for a part of this blazon).

Dukes of Orléans: France modern, a baton *argent*.

John Evelyn: *azure*, a gryphon passant

and a chief *or* (*i. e.*, both animal and chief are *or*).

Flanders: *or*, a lion rampant *sable*, armed *gules*.

Frontenac: *azure*, three eagles'gambs, 2, 1.

Greece: *azure*, a Greek cross *argent*.

Grenada: *argent*, a pomegranate *proper*.

Guienne: *gules*, a lion passant gardant *or*.

Hohenzollern: quarterly *sable* and *argent*.

Knights of St. John of Jerusalem: they bore on a chief *gules* a cross *argent*.

London: *argent*, a cross *gules*, in dexter chief a dagger, point up, *proper*.

Lords of the Isles: *argent*, a lymphad (*i. e.*, an ancient war-galley) *sable*.

Magdeburg: per fesse *gules* and *argent*, a bordure counterchanged.

Knights of Malta: *gules*, a Maltese cross *argent*.

Mar: *azure*, a bend between six crosses crosslet fitché *or*.

Percy (ancient): *azure*, a fesse engrailed (*i. e.*, with edges like Fig. 12) *or*.

Pola (city): *vert*, a cross *or*.

Sardinia: *argent*, a cross *gules*, cantoned by four Moors' heads (*i. e.*, one in each angle of the cross).

Shelley: *sable*, a fesse engrailed between three whelks (*i. e.,* shells) *or*.

Sir Philip Sidney: *or*, a pheon (*i. e.,* arrow-head) *azure*.

Sleswick: *or*, two lions passant gardant in pale (*i. e.,* one above the other) *azure*.

Stuart: *or*, a fesse checky *argent* and *azure*.

Suabia: *argent*, an eagle displayed *sable*, armed *gules*.

Thun and Taxis: *azure*, a badger *proper* (a badger in German is *Dachs*, which is a rebus for Taxis).

Tyrol: *argent*, an eagle displayed *gules*.

Ulster: *or*, a cross *gules*.

University of Bologna: *gules*, two keys *argent* in saltire; on a chief *azure* a closed book, palewise, *or*.

University of Cambridge, England: *gules*, on a cross *ermine*, between four lions of England, a book of the first (arms first used in 1580).

University of Heidelberg: *sable*, a lion rampant *or*, crowned *gules*, holding in his paws an open book.

University of Oxford: *azure*, between three open crowns *or* an open book *proper*.

Venice: *azure*, the winged lion of St. Mark *or*.

Washington (George): see the frontispiece.

Wellington (Duke of): see Fig. 52.

ARMS OF KINGDOMS AND STATES

HERALDRY is closely allied with history in the armorial bearings of kingdoms and monarchs. The evidences of the alliances of ruling kings, and even of their aspirations, are, as it were, petrified in their coats of arms. The gold noble (coin) of Edward III of England displays his arms quarterly, I and IV France ancient, II and III England, and thus exhibits two interesting facts: first, that Edward claimed the crown of France as of right; and, second, that he gave France precedence over England. And, in fact, the France which he claimed (western France, from Nantes to the Pyrenees) was then a richer inheritance than his island kingdom. The fleurs-de-lis on the tressure (fleury-counter-fleury) surrounding the lion of Scotland (see Fig. 50) mark the alliances of the Scottish and

French royal houses. The Guelfs, who had claims on the throne of England (about 1300), bore the English arms diminished, *i. e.*, *gules*, two (not three) lions of England. Their crest contains the white horse of the old Saxons over a kingly crown. The seal of Trinity College, Dublin (1591), bears the name of Queen Elizabeth and the Tudor rose (the badge of all the Tudors), but also displays the portcullis, the badge of the Beauforts, and thus exhibits a piece of early history.

The present arms of England are well known; they are quarterly, I and IV *gules*, three lions of England (*or*) in pale;[1] II Scotland (*or*, a lion rampant within a tressure fleury-counter-fleury *gules*); III Ireland (*azure*, a harp *or*, stringed *argent*). The shield is surrounded with the collar of the Garter, and surmounted by the royal crown. The crest is a lion of England. The supporters are a lion (for England) and a unicorn (for Scotland). The motto is *Dieu et mon droit.*

The full coat of arms of a monarch contains many quarterings to exhibit his many

[1] See Fig. 78.

alliances with princely houses. Whenever
the daughter of the Elector of Bavaria was
not in mourning it was a sign that "all
Europe was in good health" (court of
Louis XV).

THE SEAL, ARMS, AND FLAG OF THE UNITED STATES OF AMERICA

THE history of the great seal of the
United States is given in an official document issued by the Department of State in
1892.

Fig. 113 is a copy of the seal now in use.
It is blazoned as follows: *argent*, six pallets
gules, a chief *azure*,[1] borne on the breast of
an American eagle displayed *proper*, holding in his dexter talon an olive-branch with
thirteen fruits, in his sinister a sheaf of as
many arrows, all *proper;* above his head a
sky *azure*, charged with as many mullets
of the field, 1, 2, 3, 4, 1, environed with a
halo of rays *or*, and encircled with clouds
proper; in his beak a scroll of the last, with
the motto *E pluribus unum.*

---

[1] The arms. It should be noticed that the outer edges
of the shield are *argent;* of our flag, *gules.* Notice also
that the stars are *not* borne on the shield.

5

The Congress of the United States adopted a national flag June 14, 1777. In the early days of the Revolutionary War the different colonies made use of various banners. The national flag adopted was to have thirteen stripes (corresponding to the thirteen original States), alternately red and white (red stripes bordering the field). The Union was to be blue, charged with thirteen white stars. After various slight changes, the flag remains as above, except that the Union is now charged with as many stars as there are States. When a new State is admitted its star is added on the Fourth of July next succeeding the date of its entrance into the Union. Our flag, in this form, was first displayed on July 4, 1818.

The flag does not exactly reproduce the arms, it will be seen — nor, of course, is there any reason why it should do so. Both flag and arms are strictly heraldic. In the opinion of most persons, the flag of the United States is used too freely, and with too little respect, for advertising purposes, as a trade-mark, etc. A movement is on foot to regulate its use in such ways, and several of the States of the Union are considering laws to restrain its improper display. Such laws should be very carefully drawn so as not to impose restrictions that are merely vexatious. The more the flag is displayed the better, provided always that it is done in a respectful manner. The national coat of arms is used very freely in England, Germany, Austria, etc., with excellent results.

Besides the great seal of the United States, each of the executive departments (State, Treasury, War, Navy, etc.) has its seal; and many of the bureaus (Bureau of Navigation, Hydrographic Office, etc., in the Navy, Engineer Department in the Army, etc.) have adopted seals.

The Senate and House of Representatives also have their seals. The seal of the Treasury Department may be seen on all our paper money, the arms of the United States on our coins.

Each State of the Union has its great seal. Those of the older States are often very appropriate and well designed (as those of Massachusetts, Rhode Island, Connecticut, etc.). Many of the seals of the newer States contravene all heraldic rules, and are mere monstrosities (those of Nevada, Kansas, Minnesota, etc.). They were adopted in a stage of culture in which such things were valued simply for their legal use. From time to time real improvements are introduced (by law), and it is instructive to note that these are always returns to heraldic usage. Some of the States have adopted State flags (Connecticut in 1897, for example); and a State emblem, usually a flower, has also been chosen in many instances. Most of our cities have seals, a few of them being very well designed. A very full account of American official seals is given in Zieber's "Heraldry in America."

TITLES OF NOBILITY

THE highest hereditary title that can be held by a British subject is that of *Duke*. The premier duke of England is Henry Fitzalan Howard, Duke of Norfolk and Earl of Surrey (1483), Earl of Arundel (feudal title about 1139, confirmed 1433), Earl of Norfolk (1644), Baron Fitzalan,

Clun, and Oswaldestre (1627), Baron Maltravers (1330, by writ).

The premier duke of Scotland is Alfred Douglas Douglas-Hamilton, Duke of Hamilton and Marquess of Clydesdale (1643), Marquess of Douglas (1633), Marquess of Hamilton (1599), Earl of Selkirk (1646), Earl of Lanark, Arran, and Cambridge (1643), Earl of Angus (1389), Baron Hamilton (1445), Baron Abernethy and Jedburgh Forest (1633), Baron Avon, Polmont, Machanshire, and Innerdale (1643), Baron Daer and Shortcleuch (1646), Duke of Brandon and Baron Dutton (1712).

The premier duke of Ireland is Maurice Fitzgerald, Duke of Leinster (1766), Marquess of Kildare and Earl of Offaly (1761), Earl of Kildare (1316), Baron of Offaly (1205, by tenure). There are 22 English, 8 Scottish, and 2 Irish dukes.

The next hereditary rank is that of *Marquess*. In 1896 there were 22 English, 4 Scottish, and 10 Irish marquesses. Next in order come the *Earls* (121 English, 44 Scottish, 62 Irish titles). The Earls are followed by the *Viscounts* (29 of England, 5 of Scotland, 37 of Ireland). Then follow the *Barons* (310 of England, 25 of Scotland, 65 of Ireland).

The oldest title of Baron is held by De Courcy, Lord Kingsale, Baron Courcy, Baron of Ringrone (an Irish title of 1181, confirmed by patent in 1397, which was preceded by an English barony by tenure, from the Conquest, 1066).

The title of *Baronet* was created by James I in order to fill his treasury for the conquest of Ireland. Any gentleman with an estate of the annual value of one thousand pounds, who would agree to maintain thirty soldiers for three years in Ireland, might receive the title; and the treasury issued a receipt to him for the first year's pay of the soldiery, at the rate of eightpence per day. One of the most amusing of survivals occurs in this connection. The baronets of to-day are no longer obliged to maintain the quota of soldiers; but the treasury, to preserve the ancient form of the warrant, still issues to the newly created baronet of 1898 a receipt for the pay of thirty men for one year!

The first baronet of England (1611) was Sir Nicholas Bacon, father of Sir Francis, afterward Lord Bacon. A descendant still holds the title as eleventh baronet. There are 771 baronets of England and the United Kingdom (1896), 91 baronets of Scotland, 64 of Ireland. A baronet is " Sir Nicholas Bacon, *Bart.*," for example; his wife is " Lady " Bacon.

All the foregoing dignities are hereditary, and they are seldom conferred upon persons who have not wealth to maintain them. Personal honors are conferred upon individuals, for their lives only, by bestowing the decorations of the various orders of knighthood, as the Bath, etc. The Knight is " Sir Nicholas Bacon, K. C. B."; his wife is " Lady " Bacon. The lowest distinction is that of Knight Bachelor. It is conferred by the sovereign in person, and is personal, not hereditary. A Knight Bachelor is "Sir Nicholas Bacon, *Kt.*"; his wife is " Lady " Bacon.

The nobility of Germany is divided into different classes, as follows: (1) *Herzog* (Duke); (2) *Fürst* (Prince) (there are two classes of princes: the higher, who are addressed as *Durchlaucht;* the lower, who are styled *Fürstliche Gnaden);* (3) *Graf*

(Count); (4) *Freiherr* (Baron); (5) nobles; and this class includes the *Ritter* (Knight).

In Austria the nobles are, in order, *Herzog, Fürst, Marquis, Graf, Conte, Baron* (*Freiherr*), *Ritter*, etc.

In France, *Duc, Prince, Marquis, Comte, Vicomte, Baron, Chevalier.*

In Italy, *Duca, Principe, Marchese, Conte, Viconte, Barone, Nobile.*

In Sweden, *Graf, Baron, Adel* (noble).

In Russia the order is, Princes, Counts, Barons, and nobles.

One of the titles of the King of France was "Most Christian King"; the King of Spain is "His Catholic Majesty"; the King of Hungary "His Apostolic Majesty." Henry VIII of England received the title of "Defender of the Faith." These titles were conferred by the Pope.

ORDERS OF KNIGHTHOOD

In a small book like the present, written for Americans, little need be said of the orders of knighthood. At a diplomatic reception at the White House, or at a ball in London, the insignia of modern orders (which are worn only with full dress) may be seen. The Knight wears the jewel (usually a cross) on the left breast of the coat; the Knight Commander wears it suspended from a ribbon round the neck (*en sautoir*); the higher officers wear a star on the breast, with a wide ribbon over the shoulder. In evening dress miniatures of the orders are often worn at the buttonhole of the coat. In morning costume a ribbon or rosette may be worn, also at the buttonhole.

In former days Knights of St. John (Knights of Malta) augmented their coats of arms by a chief *gules*, charged with a cross *or;* and the Knights of the Teutonic Order bear its cross in their arms. For the higher grades of an order of knighthood the collar of the order surrounds the shield of the coat of arms, and is charged with the motto of the order, as, *Honi soit qui mal y pense* ("Shame to him who thinks evil of it") for the Garter. The lower grades (commander, knight) suspend the cross below the shield by the ribbon. In English heraldry the helmet of the knight must be in full face, not in profile.

The history of the ancient orders of chiv-

alry—the Golden Fleece (founded 1430), the
Order of St. John of Jerusalem (1048), the
Templars (1118–19), etc.—may be found
in most books of reference. Some of
the more important orders are mentioned
below, with the dates of their foundation,
etc.

England.—Order of the *Garter* (A.D. 1350).
This order, like those of the *Thistle* (1540)
and of *St. Patrick* (1783), is bestowed only
on princes and great nobles.

Order of the *Bath* (1399)—G. C. B., K. C. B.,
C. B. It is given to both soldiers and
civilians.

Order of *St. Michael and St. George*—
G. C. M. G., K. C. M. G., C. M. G. It is usually conferred for services in the colonies,
except India, which has two orders of its
own, viz., the *Star of India*, and the *Indian
Empire*—K. C. S. I., K. C. I. E., etc.

The *Victoria Cross* is not an order, properly speaking; but it is a high distinction
for military valor.

France.—The old orders of France were
swept away by the Revolution. A famous
order—the *Legion of Honor*—was instituted
by Napoleon I in 1802, and is still in exis-

tence. Its ribbon is red. Though very freely given, it is highly prized. It is bestowed on civilians as well as soldiers.

Denmark.—The Order of the *Elephant* (1190) is one of the oldest in Europe, as well as the Danish Order of the *Danebrog* (1219). The former is given only to princes and kings.

Austria.—Austria maintains an Order of the *Golden Fleece* (1430), and many other distinctions of the sort. The Order of the *Iron Crown* (of Lombardy) was instituted by Napoleon I in 1805, and has been adopted by Austria.

Prussia.—The Order of the *Black Eagle* (1701) is the highest distinction in Prussia, and its wearers are all of the higher nobility. The *Red Eagle* (1705) and the Order *pour le Mérite* (1740) are given for civil merit as well as for military service. The *Iron Cross* is given for military valor alone.

Saxony.—The kingdom of Saxony has various orders, of which the *Albert Order* (1850) is most often seen. The Saxon duchies bestow the *Ernestine Order* (1690). Both are given to civilians as well as soldiers.

Belgium.—The Order of *Leopold* (1832).

Greece.—The Order of the *Redeemer* (1829).

Italy.—The Order of the *Annunciation* (1362) is one of the most ancient of Europe, and is bestowed on princes only. The orders of *St. Maurice and St. Lazarus* (1434) and of the *Crown of Italy* (1868) are given for both military and civil merit. The Pope bestows various orders also.

Portugal has several orders, of which those of *St. Benedict of Avis* (1143), *St. James* (1170), the Order of *Christ* (1317), the *Tower and Sword* (1459), are very ancient foundations, connected with the Crusades.

Spain also has several ancient orders: *Calatrava* (about 1150), *St. James* (1170), *Alcántara* (1156), *Our Lady of Montesa* (1316), the *Golden Fleece* (1430).

Russia.—The most famous order of Russia is the *St. George* (1769), which is bestowed only for the highest military services. The orders of *St. Vladimir* (1782) and *St. Anne* (1735) are often seen.

Venezuela.—The only order maintained on the South American continent is the Order of the *Liberator* (Bolívar), which was founded by Peru in 1825 (and subsequently dissolved), and adopted by Venezuela in 1854.

United States.—The *Cincinnati* is a true order, in which the honor descends to the eldest son. It was instituted at the close of the War of the Revolution (1783). General Washington was its first president. The *Medal of Honor*, given by the United States to its soldiers and sailors, is a true decoration (see the section of this work on patriotic societies, pages 83 and 86).

SILVER PLATE

A VERY interesting chapter might be written on the silver plate of colonial times now in the possession of churches, corporations, and individuals. Much was brought here from England and the Continent (and this can usually be identified and dated by the hall-marks). From early days there were American silversmiths, of whom Paul Revere (1735–1818), who made the night-ride from Boston to Lexington (1775), is perhaps the most famous. Pieces of silverware are often marked with the initials of married couples, thus W ^{B} A, which might mean that the piece belonged to William and Agnes Blake, for instance. Many of the seventeenth-century pieces were engraved with arms when they were brought from England. In the eighteenth century it became common for prosperous gentlemen in the colonies to assume armorial bearings, which were sometimes entirely new achievements, but more often were similar to those of some branch of the family in the old country (see Fig. 119, which represents a piece of plate made in Boston before 1750).

HEREDITARY PATRIOTIC SOCIETIES IN THE UNITED STATES

WITHIN the past few years there has been a remarkable movement in the United States, which has resulted in the formation of many patriotic hereditary societies of large membership, with chapters in every State of the Union. Those only are eligible to membership who can prove their descent from an ancestor of colonial or Revolutionary times, from an officer or soldier or seaman of the various wars, from a pilgrim in the *Mayflower*, an early Huguenot emigrant, etc. These societies bring men (and women) of like traditions together, and organize them in an effective way for action. The action contemplated is patriotic—never religious or related to party politics. The general society from its headquarters issues charters to branch societies in the different States. Each State society forms an organized group of persons well known to each other, by name at least, and often personally.

Certain of the societies have been very active in preserving old monuments, buildings, landmarks, and historic documents, or in erecting tablets and monuments at historic places, or in marking the sites of battles or the graves of Revolutionary soldiers. Others have founded prizes to be given annually to school-children for essays on events in American history. Others, again, formally celebrate the nation's anniversaries. All of them foster patriotism and historical research, and teach organization —the sinking of individual desire in a common loyalty. There are probably too many such organizations at present, and more are forming. The weaker societies will, however, die; and those that remain will represent some real aspiration of their members.

The exact significance of this remarkable movement—this return to mutuality from individualism—is not yet apparent. Some of its results are already obvious. Thousands of persons in sympathy with each other have been organized. If their collective action is needed, it can be commanded. In the case of a foreign war, for example, the centers for defense, for hospital service, etc., are already in existence.[1] The path of a military dictator in the United States would never have been strewn with roses, but such societies insure the effective distribution of thorns. The larger affairs of our States and cities will undoubtedly be greatly influenced by the union of good citizens, of like traditions (and those excellent), for common and unselfish ends. Finally, the educative power of such unions, where, as has been said, loyalty to an abstraction is cultivated and individualistic aims are discouraged, is immensely important to our development as

[1] The Greek-letter fraternities of colleges could also be utilized in these ways.

a nation. They supply exactly what was needed by the country at large, and more especially by its younger and cruder portions. In what follows a brief enumeration of some of these societies will be made. It must be remembered that many of them count their membership by thousands. A note directed to any of the secretaries-general (whose addresses are here given) will bring printed circulars in return, which give more detailed information than can be printed here. It is worth while for every citizen who is eligible to make inquiries, at any rate, and to determine whether it is not desirable to join at least one of these organizations.

Each of these societies and orders has a seal (and often a flag) for the general society, as well as seals for the separate State chapters. A diploma is given to members, and each member has a right to wear the badge or decoration suspended from a ribbon of the society's color. A rosette of the colors may be worn at the buttonhole of the coat. The right to use such insignia has been protected in many States by law, and the United States has authorized its

6

officers and soldiers to wear the badges of the military and naval orders. It is sometimes flippantly said that the right to wear such insignia is the sole motive for joining the societies. This judgment is entirely superficial. The greatest satisfactions of mankind have always been found in joint action for unselfish ends. In their special way these organizations foster a common effort for ends that are thoroughly worthy.

As the entrance to such societies is through descent from some ancestor, genealogy has been powerfully stimulated, and thousands of family records have been examined and summarized in print. Our colonial and Revolutionary history has been studied in its details, which is the only way to fully realize it. The men of to-day have been connected with colonial and Revolutionary times. The children of the coming century will find their ancestral records all prepared for them, and they will be face to face with high standards of duty and effort.

A few of these societies are very exclusive, and require high social standing of their members as well as eligibility on

grounds of ancestry. The complaint has
been raised that such societies are too aris-
tocratic for a republic. The same charge
might lie against many exclusive social
or literary clubs. Such clubs and such
societies often perform a very useful part.
If they do not meet an actual want, they
will most assuredly die. If their preten-
sions are too great, they will be laughed out
of existence. The world is wide; there is
room for us all. To allow full scope to all
individualities is the mark of a strong
nation.

The Society of Colonial Wars (instituted
1892) is open to the lineal male descendants
of civil or military officers, or of soldiers,
who served the colonies between May 13,
1607 (Jamestown), and April 19, 1775 (Lexington). The address of the secretary-general is 4 Warren street, New York city.

The Society of American Wars (founded in
1897) includes the lineal male descendants
of soldiers or civil officers from 1607 to
1783, and of officers of the War of 1812, of
the War with Mexico, and of the Civil War.
The recorder's address is 500 Eighth street,
South, Minneapolis, Minnesota.

The Order of the Founders and Patriots of America (founded 1896) is open to any male citizen of the United States who is lineally descended in the male line of either parent from an ancestor who settled in any of the colonies between 1607 and 1657, and whose intermediate ancestors adhered as patriots to the cause of the colonists throughout the War of the Revolution. Secretary-general's address, 101 West Eighty-ninth street, New York city.

The Society of the Cincinnati (instituted 1783) is composed of descendants of officers of the Revolutionary army, usually the eldest male direct descendant. The address of the secretary-general is 31 Nassau street, New York city.

The Aztec Club (founded 1847) is open to the descendants of officers of the army who served in Mexico, usually the eldest male direct descendant. The secretary's address is War Department, Washington.

The Military Order of the Loyal Legion of the United States (founded 1865) is composed of officers who served in the War of the Rebellion, and of their eldest direct male lineal descendants. A letter addressed to the recorder-in-chief, Philadelphia, Pennsylvania, will be delivered.

The Military Order of Foreign Wars of the United States (instituted 1894) is composed of officers who have served in such wars, and of their lineal male descendants. Secretary-general's address, 478 Classon Avenue, Brooklyn, New York.

The Society of the War of 1812 (organized 1814) is composed of lineal male descendants of soldiers or sailors of the War of 1812. General secretary's address, Germantown, Pennsylvania.

The Naval Order of the United States (instituted 1890) is open to officers of the navy who have served in war, and to their male descendants, etc., and also to enlisted men who have received a Medal of Honor from the United States for bravery. Secretary's address, Navy Department, Washington.

The Sons of the American Revolution (instituted 1875) must prove their descent from a Revolutionary ancestor. **The Sons of the Revolution** (1876) is organized on the same basis. It is expected that these two large societies will soon be consolidated. Secretary-general, S. A. R., 143 Chestnut

street, Newark, New Jersey. Secretary-
general, S. R., 146 Broadway, New York city.

The Holland Society (incorporated in 1775)
is composed of the direct male descendants
of Hollanders resident in America before
1675. Secretary's address, 346 Broadway,
New York city.

The Huguenot Society of America (organized 1883) admits descendants of Huguenots
who came to America before 1787. General
secretary's address, 105 East Twenty-second
street, New York city.

The Society of Colonial Dames of America
(organized 1891) is composed of women
descended from an ancestor who held an
office of importance in the colonies previous
to 1750. The secretary-general's address is
825 St. Paul street, Baltimore, Maryland.

There are various other societies for
women, of which the most important are
Daughters of the American Revolution (1890)
(1710 I street, Washington, D. C.), and
Daughters of the Revolution (1891) (128 West
Fifty-ninth street, New York city), etc.;
and there is also a society of **Children of the
American Revolution** (1895) (902 F street,
Washington, D. C.).

The Society of "Mayflower" Descendants (organized 1894) includes male and female descendants of the passengers of the *Mayflower* (1620). General-secretary's address, 228 West Seventy-fifth street, New York city.

Medal of Honor Legion.—The one decoration that is given by the government of the United States is the *Medal of Honor*, which was authorized by acts of Congress of 1862 and 1863 to be awarded to officers and enlisted men of the army for "gallantry in action and soldier-like qualities during the present insurrection." It has been bestowed only for conspicuous services. For example, the Twenty-seventh Regiment of Maine Infantry was present on the field where the battle of Gettysburg was fought, and its term of service had expired. The entire regiment, to a man, volunteered to remain on the field and to fight the battle; and for this gallant conduct a medal was awarded to each officer and man. A *Naval Medal of Honor* is also awarded by the government, and it is highly prized. The United States also authorizes its officers and men to wear the decorations of those patriotic hereditary societies which commemorate service in any of the wars of the nation (not those of the colonies).

There are a number of other societies, formed or forming, which are not mentioned here for lack of space.

HOW TO TRACE A PEDIGREE

CANDIDATES for membership in any of the hereditary societies are required to furnish a written pedigree showing their descent from some ancestor in Revolutionary or colonial times. For each person in the line to be traced back there should be given (1) the full name, (2) the date of birth, (3) the date of marriage, (4) the date of death; and it is desirable to know for each male ancestor, (5) his place of residence, (6) his civil or military service, etc.

These data should be obtained from living persons for as many generations back as is practicable. Documents in the possession of one's family may serve to carry the pedigree further. Finally, recourse must be had to town, county, and State records, and to genealogical books and publications.

It will often be the simplest way to apply
direct to some professional genealogist,[1]
and to make an arrangement by which the
missing links are to be looked up.

It is always more instructive and interesting to do this work one's self among the
family histories of a large library. Several
of the States (Massachusetts is a striking
example) have their colonial and Revolutionary records admirably arranged, so that
the original documents (rosters, deeds, wills,
etc.), or copies of them, may be readily consulted. All public libraries have many
works on genealogy, and the librarians are
prepared to give needed advice. A little
perseverance, and a little system in keeping
one's notes, will usually bring out what is
needed. After the data are obtained, it is
very necessary to arrange them in an orderly form. Whitmore's Ancestral Tablets
are well suited for such a purpose. These
general directions are all that need be given
here. The particular methods of research
and the special books to be consulted are

[1] Addresses of such experts may be found on the advertising pages of the publications of genealogical and
historical or patriotic societies.

different for different States. It is the business of the librarian or of the expert to put one on the track, and it is not difficult to follow it if one has access to the books.

ANCIENT LINEAGE

THE Egyptians have possessed written records for something like six thousand years. There might conceivably be a pedigree as long as this. A very little acquaintance with the history of dynasties or of families shows that a proved descent of a thousand years is a marvel, and that one of two thousand is unknown in Europe. This brings us to ask, What is ancient lineage? Mr. Samuel Pepys, who knew a little of everything, was in conversation with the Garter King-at-arms of his day (November 11, 1664), who "in discourse did say that there was none of the families of princes in Christendom that do derive themselves so high as Julius Cæsar, nor so far by a thousand years, that can directly prove their rise; only some in Germany do derive themselves from the patrician families of Rome, but that uncertainly; and he did much inveigh against the writing of romances, that five hundred years hence being writ of things in general true, the world will not know which is true and which is false."

Since Pepys's time genealogy has become an exact science, and precise data are available. Among the barons of Great Britain, Lord Kingsale can trace the possession of his English lands to the Conquest, and Lord Wrottesley to within a century of that time; Lord Sudeley in France to the Counts of Vexin in the tenth century, etc. The Danish sculptor Thorwaldsen claimed a proved descent from one of the Icelanders who returned from the discovery of America (A. D. 1000), etc. Mar was a powerful mormaership before St. Columba came to Scotland (A. D. 563), and its lord was one of the seven earls of Scotland. The descent is proved from 1093, step by step. About A. D. 609 King Ethelbert of Kent granted lands in Essex to the church, on condition that the income should go to old St. Paul's in London (founded by St. Austin before 607), and the same land is still held by the church. This is the oldest tenure in England, and probably in Europe.

All over the Orient, in Mohammedan countries, one meets with descendants of the Prophet (who was born in A. D. 570). It is probable that there are many pretenders to this honor; but it is certain that there are hundreds and hundreds of persons whose claims are entirely authentic, and whose descent is carefully registered by the chief of the family, who has his seat in Mecca. Such a lineage is ancient, beyond a doubt. In China, where the tablets of ancestors are preserved in a family hall and periodically honored, descent can be traced for centuries without a break. The descendants of Confucius (born B. C. 551) are hereditary nobles to-day. Among the Jews, too, especially the Jews of Spain and the East, and in Venice, Bosnia, and Bulgaria, genealogies of many centuries are common. The Mikado of Japan was the religious head of his nation as well as its ruler. The dignity is hereditary, and has remained in one family since the time of Nebuchadnezzar (B. C. 660). Here is the most ancient lineage known, though it includes adopted sons. The present Emperor of Japan is the one hundred and twenty-second of his line. There are few religions as old as this dynasty.

Among Western nations, poverty extending over two or three generations, seems effectively to extinguish family pride, except, perhaps, in parts of Spain, where the common laborer may have the ancient coat of arms of his house built in among the stones of his hovel. Certainly in England and America poverty soon effaces all knowledge or interest of the sort.

Ancient lineage of the kind known to Moslems is the rarest thing in our Western world. Of the English barons in the House of Lords (some five hundred in number) there are less than a dozen whose baronies date back to 1400, and the earliest is 1264. The Moslem Seiyid goes eight centuries further back, to the great-grandfather of Mohammed (A. D. 472), or even, if we are to believe the commentators, to Adnan (B. C. 122). There are less than a dozen English peerages of the fifteenth century even. The vast majority have been created since 1700 for services in war, on the bench, or at the bar, or for landed power and influence. The same thing, in a less degree, is

true of the princely and ducal houses of the
Continent. There are comparatively few
of the German counts whose titles date back
to the sixteenth century. In 1863 the House
of Lords had not a single descendant of any
of the barons who were chosen to enforce
Magna Charta (1215), nor of any one who
fought against the French at Agincourt
(1415).

The Almanach de Gotha is a trustworthy
guide to the genealogies of the princely
houses of Europe. The house of Hapsburg
springs from Gontran the Rich,[1] Count of
Altenburg, whose seat was in Switzerland,
A. D. 952. His descendants first became
Counts of Hapsburg, 1020; Kings of Germany, 1273; Dukes of Austria, 1282; Kings
of the Romans and Emperors of Germany,
1519, etc. The ancestor of the Bourbons
was Robert the Strong,[1] Count of Anjou,
864; Count of Paris and Orléans, 866; his
son Eudes became King of France in 888.
The Bourbons of Spain date from 1700.
The house of Hohenzollern has its origin
in the marriage of Friedrich, Count of Zol-

[1] Riches and strength have been the sources of power
and rank from time immemorial.

lern (1192–1200), with the heiress of the
Counts of Nuremberg. It was not till 1411
that a branch of this house was called to
govern the mark of Brandenburg. In 1520
they were Dukes of Prussia, and assumed
the title of kings so late as 1701. It is interesting to remark that the right to bear
the present crest of the Hohenzollerns (a
dog's head, quarterly *argent* and *sable*) was
purchased for a large sum of money in
1317.

Every one remembers the pleasing tale
of that Prince of Croy whose painting of
the deluge represented Noah bearing into
the ark a precious box labeled " Records of
the family of Croy "; and yet this ancient
family appears " authentically " only in
1207. The family of the Chancellor of the
German Empire, Hohenlohe, has borne that
name since 1182, but is still more ancient.
The Metternichs date from 1350. The famous family of Montmorency has for "probable origin " an ancestor in 1214; it is
tradition only that carries them back to
the Seigneur of St. Denis in 998. Talley-
rand dates from 1199; Harcourt appears
authentically in 1024; Bismarck in 1270;

the Rohans (by that name) in 1128; Broglie in 1254; Gramont in 1381; Doria in 1335; Borghese in 1450; La Rochefoucauld in 1019; Graham (Dukes of Montrose) in 1128; Noailles in 1230; Poniatowski in 1142; Choiseul in 1060; Radziwill in 1412; Richelieu in 1596; Grosvenor (Dukes of Westminster) in 1066; St. Maur (Dukes of Somerset) in 1240; Corsini in 1170; Rocca in 1102.

The Colonnas were a patrician family of Rome, from which came, according to tradition, four popes of Rome between the years 300 and 884. Genealogically speaking, their origin is not proved beyond 1100. The Orsini are descended from another patrician family, from which issued, according to tradition, two popes (A. D. 752 and 757). The popes elected in 1191 and 1277 did certainly belong to this ancient and powerful family, which traces its authentic origin to a senator of Rome in 1190.

The foregoing are some of the oldest names in Europe, specially selected out of long lists that include hundreds of later origin. The dates of the dukes of Napoleon's creation—Ney, Murat, Lannes, Berthier—look very modern beside those of the Montmorencys and Turennes; but they are all in the lists for the same reason—for magnificent services rendered to their country.

The Almanach de Gotha has only room for kings and princes; but a reference to any book on the landed gentry (of England or of the Tyrol, for example) would show that long descents are by no means confined to the peers, and that there are very few really ancient lineages. If one is allowed to count the stream of blood as it runs through female as well as male ancestors, the list of long descents is much increased by reckoning the marriages with the daughters of kings. Count Albert de Mun, the Catholic socialist, and leader of the "Right" in the French Assembly, descends (through females) from Clovis the Great (born A. D. 465), and from the grandfather of Clovis, Merovæus, from whom the Merovingian kings derive their name. Here is an ancestry which puts that of the Bourbons (who do not even go back to Charlemagne) to shame, and it is, without doubt, the longest proved pedigree of the Western world.

7

If such descents in the female line are counted, England and America possess many long pedigrees, not a few of which are derived from descents from the daughters of the Scottish kings, and may be traced back to Kenneth I (died 860), or to Kenneth's ancestor Fergus, who crossed from Ireland to Britain in A. D. 503. Many Irish pedigrees are portentously long, also.

It is practically impossible to trace descents other than those of royal personages further back than the eleventh century, except in one special class of cases. When funds have been left with religious bodies for the saying of masses for the souls of ancestors, it is sometimes possible to connect them with their descendants. It was not until the eleventh and twelfth centuries, indeed, that an individual was known by a surname. An individual known by one name only is identified with difficulty, except under very special circumstances. Consider how much labor has been expended on the pedigree of Shakspere or of Washington, and how little, comparatively, has been learned.

In America there is an astonishing num-

ber of families that can trace their descent
from the first emigrant, and comparatively
few which can prove their descent from an
English ancestor. The first settlers, especially of New England, kept excellent
records of all their public transactions.
Our public records have been, on the
whole, admirably preserved, and the genealogical and patriotic societies throughout
the country, as well as the governments of
several States, have provided against their
loss by reprinting many of them. It is not
a little remarkable how easy it is to trace
the growth of a family from the seventeenth century down to the War of the
Revolution; and as Americans in general
have a decided taste for genealogy, the re-
sult has been a vast library of such family
histories. Family pride of a perfectly
legitimate sort has thus been stimulated,
and this can never grow to be a dangerous
thing in a republic. In fact, it is an admirable lesson to learn to prize something
less tangible than stocks and bonds. Moreover, people in general have thus learned
that there are hundreds of families as good
as their own, and this is also an excellent

thing to realize. Tradition tells us that the
Laird of Macnab refused to acknowledge
his descent from Noah (" the Macnabs had a
boat of their own "), because he was used to
live in a small community without equals.

INDEX TO HERALDIC TERMS

THE titles to the separate figures in the
following plates contain nearly all heraldic
terms in common use.[1]

[1] For formal definitions of these terms the reader may
consult the Century Dictionary, in which they are given
with much fullness, or any of the other large dictionaries.

7*

PLATES

PLATE I

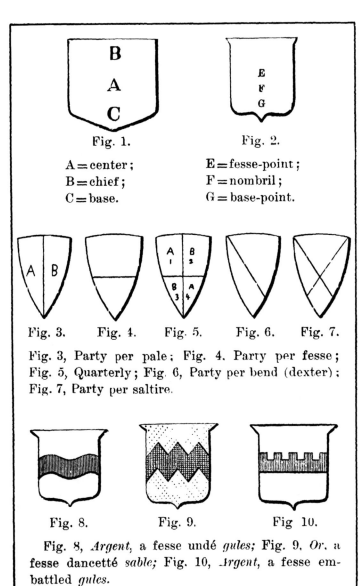

Fig. 1.

A = center ;
B = chief ;
C = base.

Fig. 2.

E = fesse-point ;
F = nombril ;
G = base-point.

Fig. 3.   Fig. 4.   Fig. 5.   Fig. 6.   Fig. 7.

Fig. 3, Party per pale ; Fig. 4. Party per fesse ;
Fig. 5, Quarterly ; Fig. 6, Party per bend (dexter) ;
Fig. 7, Party per saltire.

Fig. 8.   Fig. 9.   Fig 10.

Fig. 8, *Argent*, a fesse undé *gules;* Fig. 9. *Or*, a
fesse dancetté *sable;* Fig. 10, *Argent*, a fesse embattled *gules.*

PLATE II

Fig. 11.   Fig. 12.   Fig. 13.

Fig. 11, *Argent*, a fesse nebulé *gules*.

Fig. 12, *Argent*, a bend engrailed *gules*.

Fig 13, *Argent*, a pale "invected" *gules*.

Fig. 14.   Fig. 15.   Fig. 16.

Fig. 14, *Argent*, a pale *azure*.

Fig. 15, Paly of six, *argent* and *gules*.

Fig. 16, Per pale *gules* and *argent*, three roundels counterchanged, two and one.

Fig. 17.   Fig. 18.   Fig. 19.

Fig. 17. Per pale *gules* and *or*, a boar passant counterchanged.

Fig. 18, *Or* (gold).

Fig. 19, *Gules* (red).

PLATE III

Fig. 20. Fig. 21. Fig. 22.

Fig. 20, *Azure* (blue).
Fig. 21. *Sable* (black).
Fig. 22, *Vert* (or *sinople*) (green).

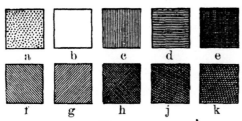

Fig. 23.

Fig. 23, The tinctures: a. *or* (gold); b, *argent* (silver); c, *gules* (red); d, *azure* (blue); e, *sable* (black); f, *vert* (green); g, *purpure* (purple); h, *sanguine* or *murrey* (blood-red); j, k, *tenné* or *tenney* (tawny, orange).

Fig. 24. Fig. 25. Fig. 26.

Fig. 24. *Ermine.*
Fig. 25, *Vair.*
Fig. 26, *Potent.*

PLATE IV

Fig. 27.   Fig. 28.   Fig. 29.

Fig 27, *Erminois*.
Fig. 28, *Pean*.
Fig. 29, *Ermines*.

Fig. 30.   Fig. 31.   Fig. 32.

Fig. 30, *Argent*, a chief *gules*.
Fig. 31, *Argent*, a bend (dexter) *azure*.
Fig. 32, A sword bendwise.

Fig. 33.   Fig. 34.   Fig. 35.

Fig. 33, A lion rampant "debruised" by a bendlet.
Fig. 34, *Argent*, a baton sinister, coupé, *gules* (the mark of illegitimate descent).
Fig. 35, *Argent*, a fesse *gules*.

PLATE V

Fig. 36.

Fig. 36 bis.

Fig. 37.

Fig. 36, *Argent*, a bar *gules*.
Fig. 36 bis, *Argent*, a chevron *gules*.
Fig. 37, *Argent*, a saltire *azure*.

Fig. 37 bis.

Fig. 38.

Fig. 39.

Fig. 37 bis, *Azure*, a saltire voided *argent*.
Fig. 38, *Argent*, a cross *gules* (St. George).
Fig. 39, A cross crosslet *gules*.

Fig. 40.

Fig. 41.

Fig. 42.

Fig. 40, A cross raguly.
Fig. 41, Anchored cross.
Fig. 42, A cross bottony *or*.

PLATE VI

Fig. 43.   Fig. 44.

Fig. 43, *Argent*, a cross cleché *vert*.
Fig. 44, A cross patté fitché.

Fig. 45.

Fig. 45, Three crosses fitché *gules*.

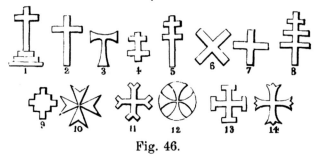

Fig. 46.

Fig. 46, Crosses: 1, Cross of Calvary; 2, Latin
cross; 3, Tau-cross (like the Greek letter *tau*); 4,
Lorraine cross; 5, Patriarchal cross; 6, St. Andrew's
cross (a saltire); 7, St. George's cross = Greek cross;
8, Papal cross; 9, Cross nowy quadrant; 10, Maltese
cross; 11, Cross fourché; 12, Cross formé or patté;
13, Cross potent (the arms of Jerusalem); 14, Cross
flory.

PLATE VII

Fig. 47.   Fig. 48.   Fig. 49.

Fig. 47, A canton dexter.
Fig. 48. Gyronny of eight, *gules* and *argent*.
Fig. 49, A bordure compony *argent* and *gules*.

Fig. 50.   Fig. 51.

Fig. 50, A double tressure fleury-counter-fleury.
Fig. 51, Quarterly: I and IV of the paternal ancestor; II and III of allied families.

PLATE VIII

Fig. 52.

Fig. 53.

Fig. 52. Arms of the first Duke of Wellington, with the augmentation of honor granted to him, viz., an inescutcheon of England.

Fig. 53, The sun in his splendor.

Fig. 54.

Fig. 55.

Fig. 54, A shield semé of fleurs-de-lis (arms of ancient France).

Fig. 55, A lion sejant affronté (the royal crest of Scotland).

PLATE IX

Fig. 56.   Fig. 57.   Fig. 58.

Fig. 56, *Gules*, a chevron accompanied by three crosses *argent*, two and one.

Fig. 57, Quarterly: I and IV *argent*, a chevron *gules;* II and III *gules*, a cross *argent*.

Fig. 58, *Or*, flanched *gules*.

Fig. 59.   Fig. 60.   Fig. 61.

Fig. 59, *Argent*, in chief three billets *azure*.

Fig. 60, *Argent*, a fusil *azure*.

Fig. 61, Barry of six, *argent* and *gules*.

Fig. 62.   Fig. 63.

Fig. 62, Checky *azure* and *argent*.

Fig. 63, Paly bendy *argent* and *gules*.

PLATE X

Fig. 64, Arms of De Berghes, from Albrecht Dürer's
original. ("D'or au lion de gueules armé d'azur:
Cimier [crest] un coq d'or crêté et barbé de gueules.")

PLATE XI

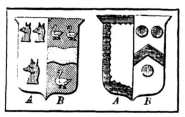

Fig. 65.   Fig. 66.

Fig. 65, The arms of the wife (B, B) impaled with those of the husband (A, A).

Fig. 66, The mound.

Fig. 67.   Fig. 68.   Fig. 69.

Fig. 67, A lion statant gardant.

Fig. 68, A lion passant regardant.

Fig. 69, A lion rampant.

Fig. 70.   Fig. 71.   Fig 72.

Fig. 70, A lion salient.

Fig. 71, A lion sejant.

Fig. 72, A lion dormant.

PLATE XII

Fig. 73. Fig. 74. Fig 74 bis

Fig. 73, Two lions combatant.

Fig. 74, A lion's head couped.

Fig. 74 bis, A lion's head erased.

Fig. 75. Fig. 76. Fig. 77.

Fig. 75, A demi-lion.

Fig. 76, A lion issuant.

Fig. 77, *Argent*, out of a fesse *gules* a demi-lion naissant *proper*.

Fig. 78.

Fig. 78, Three lions passant gardant in pale (the escutcheon of England).

PLATE XIII

Fig. 79.   Fig. 80.   Fig. 81.

Fig. 79, A dragon passant.
Fig. 80, A wivern.
Fig. 81, A cockatrice.

Fig. 82.   Fig. 83.   Fig. 84.

Fig. 82, A hart at gaze.
Fig. 83, A hart at speed.
Fig. 84, A stag courant.

Fig. 85.   Fig. 86.   Fig. 87.

Fig. 85, A stag trippant.
Fig. 86, A stag's head caboshed.
Fig. 87, An eagle displayed.

PLATE XIV

Fig. 88.　　　　Fig. 89.　　　　Fig. 90.

Fig. 88, An eagle descendent.
Fig. 89, A martlet.
Fig. 90, A dove close.

Fig. 91.　　　　Fig. 92.　　　　Fig. 93.

Fig. 91. A bird volant.
Fig. 92, A dolphin haurient.
Fig. 93, Two dolphins adorsed.

Fig. 94.　　　　Fig. 95.　　　　Fig. 96.

Fig. 94, A fish natant.

Fig 95, *Argent*, a heart *gules*, ensigned with a royal crown (part of the arms of Douglas).

Fig. 96, A crescent.

PLATE XV

Fig. 97.   Fig. 98.   Fig. 100.

Fig. 97, Three crescents interlaced (device of Diana of Poitiers).

Fig. 98, A star (estoile).

Fig. 100, The manche.

Fig. 99.   Fig. 102.

Fig. 99, Two forms of water-budgets.

Fig. 102, *Or*, a label of three points *argent*.

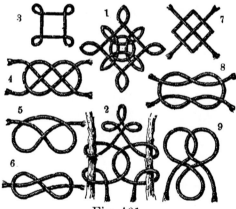

Fig. 101.

Fig. 101, Knots: 1, Lacy knot; 2, Dacre; 3, Bowen; 4, Wake (Ormond); 5, Stafford; 6, Knot of Savoy (Order of the Annunciation); 7, Harrington (or true-love) knot; 8, Bouchier; 9, Heneage knot.

PLATE XVI

Fig. 103.

Fig. 103, The royal crown of England.

Fig. 104.

Fig. 104: 1, The crown of Charlemagne; 2, The Austrian crown; 3, The Russian crown; 4, The French crown.

PLATE XVII

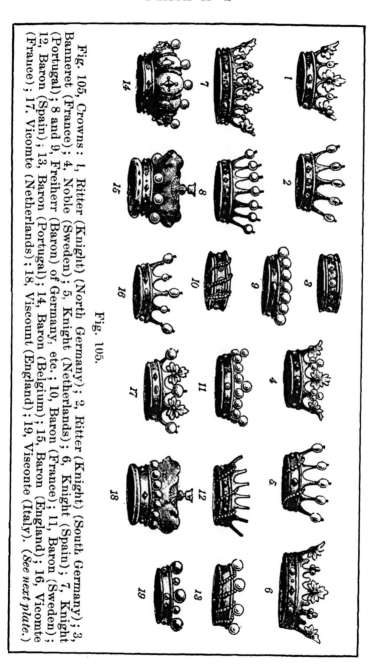

Fig. 105.

Fig. 105, Crowns : 1, Ritter (Knight) (North Germany) ; 2, Ritter (Knight) (South Germany) ; 3, Banneret (France) ; 4, Noble (Sweden) ; 5, Knight (Netherlands) ; 6, Knight (Spain) ; 7, Knight (Portugal) ; 8 and 9, Freiherr (Baron) of Germany, etc. ; 10, Baron (France) ; 11, Baron (Sweden) ; 12, Baron (Spain) ; 13, Baron (Portugal) ; 14, Baron (Belgium) ; 15, Baron (England) ; 16, Vicomte (France) ; 17, Vicomte (Netherlands) ; 18, Viscount (England) ; 19, Visconte (Italy). (See next plate.)

PLATE XVIII

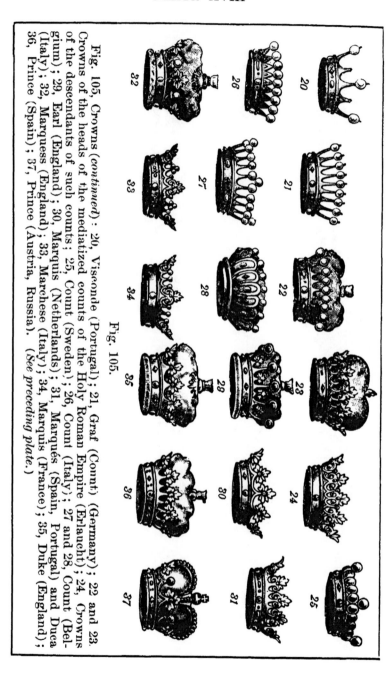

Fig. 105.

Fig. 105, Crowns (continued) : 20, Visconde (Portugal) ; 21, Graf (Count) (Germany) ; 22 and 23, Crowns of the heads of the mediatized counts of the Holy Roman Empire (Erlaucht) ; 24, Crowns of the descendants of such counts ; 25, Count (Sweden) ; 26, Count (Italy) ; 27 and 28, Count (Belgium) ; 29, Earl (England) ; 30, Marquis (Netherlands) ; 31, Marqués (Spain, Portugal) and Duca (Italy) ; 32, Marquess (England) ; 33, Marchese (Italy) ; 34, Marquis (France) ; 35, Duke (England) ; 36, Prince (Spain) ; 37, Prince (Austria, Russia). (See preceding plate.)

PLATE XIX

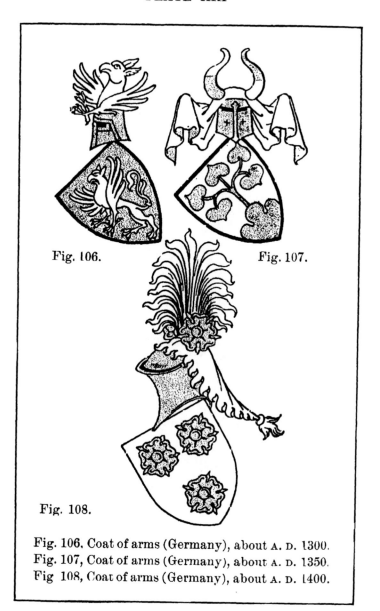

Fig. 106.

Fig. 107.

Fig. 108.

Fig. 106, Coat of arms (Germany), about A. D. 1300.
Fig. 107, Coat of arms (Germany), about A. D. 1350.
Fig. 108, Coat of arms (Germany), about A. D. 1400.

PLATE XX

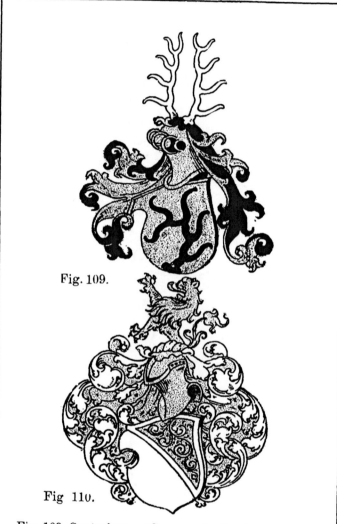

Fig. 109.

Fig 110.

Fig. 109, Coat of arms (Germany), about A. D. 1450.
Fig. 110, Coat of arms (Germany), about A. D. 1500.

PLATE XXI

Fig 111.

Fig. 112.

Fig. 111, Coat of arms (Germany), about A. D. 1650.
Fig. 112, Coat of arms (Germany), about A. D. 1750.

PLATE XXII

Fig. 113.

Fig. 115

Fig. 114.

Fig. 113, Great seal of the United States of America.

Fig. 114, Seal of the Astronomical Society of the Pacific.

Fig. 115, Seal of the Smithsonian Institution.

PLATE XXIII

Fig. 116, Seal of the Johns Hopkins University
(the quartered shield is that of Lord Baltimore).

Fig. 117, Seal of Harvard University.

PLATE XXIV

Fig. 118, Seal of the United States Department of Agriculture.

Fig. 119, A piece of silver plate made in New England about 1750.

CPSIA information can be obtained at www.ICGtesting.com
Printed in the USA
BVOW01s2327111114

374720BV00024B/290/P